Our Voices / Our Lives

Stories of Women from Central America and the Caribbean

✳

Our Voices /
Our Lives

Stories of Women from
Central America and
the Caribbean

*

Margaret Randall

Common Courage   Monroe, Maine

Library of Congress Cataloging in Publication Data
Randall, Margaret, 1936-
Our voices, our lives: stories of women from Central America
and the Caribbean/ Margaret Randall.
p. cm.
Includes index.
ISBN 1-56751-047-7, --ISBN 1-56751-046-9 (pbk.)
1. Women--Central America--Social conditions.
2. Women--Caribbean Area--Social conditions.
3. Feminism--Central America. 4.--Caribbean Area. I. Title.
HQ1467.R36 1995
305.42'09729--dc20   94-44006
CIP

Common Courage Press
Box 702
Monroe, ME 04951
207-525-0900
fax: 207-525-3068

First Printing

5/11/97

Para mi madre,

Pensé en ti cuando vi
este libro. El mismo título
me hizo ~~pensar~~ recordar la ~~de la~~
fuerza de tu voz cuando me hablas
de la vida. Tus experiencias,
tus ideas, tus consejos — todo
~~las veces cuando~~ lo
contaste
me ~~hablaste~~ de como ser una
~~mujer buena~~
y fuerte. Tu mamá me
enseñaste como ser una mujer
fuerte en la mente y sensible
en el corazón.

Tu voz hace mi vida.

Mil besos,
tu hija que te
adora, Inga

for Gladys Zalaquette: dear friend,
it's a long long road.

"The cost of a one-way fare is life."
    —Paul Monette

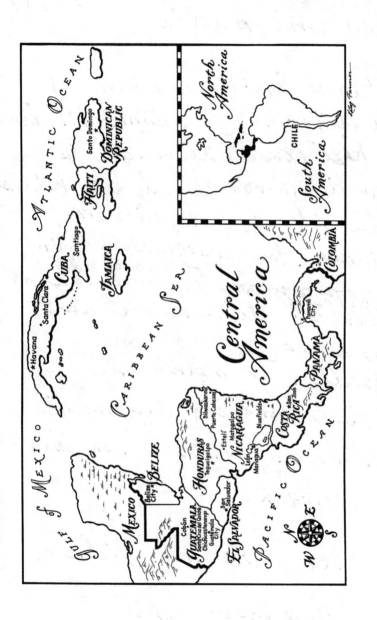

Contents

Introduction

✳

The end-of-history theory came from neoconservatives who saw in the defeat of European communism a triumph for the glories of institutionalized inequality. Fundamentalist Christians, Jews, Muslims, and other religious fanatics proceeded to rearrange the history that of course continues to unfold, using their own crazed symbolism in support of anti-life positions. The U.S. media establishment has become a kingdom unto itself, battering into self-fulfilling prophesy the bunglings of an administration seeped in maybe. Meanwhile women—for whom life is primary and history necessarily ongoing—push ahead in a revolution barely discernible to some, earth-shaking for those who choose to see.

This small book brings together a number of disparate essays and conversations, all written in the early 1990s. Some were published in earlier versions elsewhere. Most were difficult to place. They weren't the right length, or didn't say the expected. One was dubbed too political by several editors. These pieces range from Guatemala and Belize to Cuba and Nicaragua, from Chile to the Dominican Republic. What serves as connective tissue and can be heard throughout like some common energy source are the voices of women. Women speak here of their experience. They reveal a time of dramatic change and project the future from a particularly twentieth century ability to theorize out of practice.

Most of these women are feminists, meaning they share a world view about power and their own role as women. They are Central American and Caribbean feminists speaking to and with a feminist from the United States. So feminism informs these conversations and narratives. Whatever our culture orexperience, whatever the language we speak, our lives themselves attest to the fact that we do not believe in history screeching to a halt. We unequivocally reject traditionalist ideologies that would sacrifice us (or anyone else) to male conceptions of power.

In many of the Marxist experiments, women saw the State assume a new level of responsibility for that labor—undervalued and unpaid—which has long been assigned to us. Lip service and in some cases real attention was given us as protagonists in the struggle for a new society. Universal education and health care ceased to be bargaining chips about which politicians could argue while we and our children died. Our right to control our bodies was respected.

But governments of men still parceled out this recognition of women's roles. Patriarchy continued to function under socialism; the androcentric disbalance of power remained firmly entrenched. Misogyny—as well as racism, heterosexism, ageism, and models of class status or elitism—continued to go unchallenged. Criticism was avoided as dangerous and divisive. Psychological exploration was too often seen as bourgeois; collective (historic) memory was valued but the individual memories of endemic abuse were left safely untapped. Questions about sexuality, especially those that challenged patriarchal values, were ignored or silenced.

Under socialism, workers supposedly ran the factories, but it was a working-class party defending their interests, making decisions in their name. And this seems one of the more obvious problems with socialism as it developed in the old Soviet Union, in Europe, and further west: the different social groups were spoken *for*, rather than permitted to speak for themselves. Leninism had given us parties that worked on the principle of democratic centralism, and as they became institutionalized their centralism outweighed their attempts at democracy.

Women, particularly, were stifled—even as improvements in their social condition were made on their behalf. Whenever women themselves began to develop an alternative discourse, whenever and wherever indigenous feminist movements surfaced, their protagonists were quickly repressed, accused of importing "bourgeois ideas from the more industrialized countries," of dividing working-class unity and endangering the revolutionary process (which was often under attack from outside forces).

Women don't fare much better—only differently—in the capitalist world. Certainly there has been more freedom, at least among the leisure classes. Righteous anger has achieved some degree of public outlet. Activism and theory have spawned a new consciousness. New legislation has benefitted women in the workplace and in other arenas. Feminist and gender studies have gained a place (albeit a vulnerable one) in the academy.

But there is also more freedom to manipulate women's bodies to titillate male egos and to satisfy an exaltation of violence. Our body images, cut and pasted to fit whatever the market bears, become prime movers and sellers of merchandize. We ourselves are the largest targeted population whose created needs urge us on to buy, thereby helping to sustain the systems of our own oppression.

Our serious challenges to women's unpaid labor in the home and discrimination elsewhere have been joined by deeper analyses of power relations in general: beginning with a rejection of Freud's ideas about fantasy and hysteria. Our movement has not developed homogeneously. There are socialist feminists and separatist feminists, Marxist feminists and academic feminists, lesbian feminists and many other divisions. We have produced feminist social scientists and feminist literary critics. Feminist poets and writers have helped us retrieve our oldest language and develop one that is passionately new. Feminists create a new theology, talk about pornography, advocate for and against sadomasochism, have children in one- or two-mother families, fight to keep abortion legal, mythologize and demystify, mentor and learn.

Feminism's reevaluation of centuries of woman-abuse has been among the most important and far-reaching of its contributions. It has shaped new schools of psychology that have helped all people—men as well as women—see ourselves more holistically. Once we remembered what had been done to us—what is done to us still, under the guise of patriarchy and protected by a misguided sense of propriety—a great many threads come together. We begin to understand the important connections between the emotional stunting that reproduces itself from generation to generation and our difficulty in developing formulae for social change that are successful and can be sustained.

These connections are what those in power most fear, for they threaten the current status quo—in which the owners get richer, laborers are exploited in the few jobs they still retain, gender and difference carry stigma rather than possibility, sexuality is reduced to an "acceptable" expression that fortifies patriarchy, and technology is harnessed to assure further inequality rather than the bounty it is capable of providing.

As an extension of the way women have come to question the prevailing models, we also talk—and listen—to one another differently. The first piece in this book emerged from a radical approach to information-gathering. Rather than travel to places inhabited by others, on fact-finding missions that reduce experience to disembodied phrases and statistics in a reporter's notebook, ten North American women from diverse cultures chose to travel in a group representative of our national diversity. In Guatemala we wanted to tell our life stories to the women we met, and to listen to theirs. This allowed us to honor and attempt to understand difference, even as we recognized commonalities such as repeated patterns of abuse, denial, and the strengths that make us survivors.

In Guatemala we spoke with maids, religious sisters, union organizers, housewives, members of sewing cooperatives, a Mayan priestess, and women who walked through the mountains for days to meet with us for an afternoon. They talked to us about alcoholism, battery, exploitation, and memory. About their richly embroidered dress, their cultural identities, the racism and repression that plague their lives, and their hopes for a different future. Many of the Guatemalan women with whom we met live in daily fear for their lives. They are engaged in a struggle that is five centuries old. Most did not wish to be taped or photographed. The quotes, then, are not direct (verbatim), but largely remembered, *felt:* an interpretation backed up by many years of experience on the part of the listener (myself), a shared recognition of the forces of oppression, and an openness to the reenergized language of witness.

It is important to understand that this is a whole new practice of telling, a deeply feminist practice (one that most male and even many female "experts" do not trust). Not only what we say but how we speak. And how we listen. Implicit, often explicit, is a more egalitarian concept of power.

And I want to say a few things about the language of witness. In Latin America and throughout the ravaged world it has developed primarily out of liberation theology, a phenomenon which began with the Catholic Church's mid-twentieth-century recognition of itself as part of rather than outside history.

Christian communities began reading the bible in relation to their own impoverished lives. They came to understand the forces that shape those lives within the context of biblical reference. In one of the world's most patriarchal institutions, a rigid hierarchy was being challenged from the ground up. Although they had none of the power (indeed were treated as maidservants to the male god, his divine son, and the earthly preservers of tradition—also male), women in the Church played an important role in beginning to break with oppressive power structures.

Religious sisters and lay women had long been responsible for the steady work of educating future generations in values of devotion, piety, and service. Now they had questions. Tabus began falling away. Class struggle ripped through the churches as though society as a whole, leaving the fundamentalists to protect the interests of wealth while the newly-named Church of the Poor defends ordinary women and men.

Christian Base Communities grew into a vast network: multiplying the power of consciousness-raising and ultimately becoming involved in political action and revolutionary struggle. In Latin America, where there weren't enough priests to serve rural areas, modern volunteers called Delegates of the Word took over all but the holiest of sacraments. Many women became Delegates. Women as well as men have been targets of counterrevolutionary violence.

In countries like Nicaragua, Haiti, Brazil, Guatemala, and El Salvador the rapid growth of Christian social consciousness paralleled and eventually intersected with the development of indigenous political movements for social change. Revolutionaries within the Church and those who came from the more secular Communist or Socialist traditions realized they were fighting for the same thing: justice in the here and now (as well as in a hereafter that might or might not exist). Although most of the new theologians are men—logical in a structure that is still eminently male-controlled—women are often those involved in its daily practice.

In this process which already has its quarter-century of history, many religious sisters as well as lay women are questioning the Church's strictures on their right to stand up to abuse, their decisions to bear children, even their sexual choices. Increasing numbers of Catholic nuns are leaving orders where they've spent years of their lives. But these departures aren't the simple trade-off of a cloistered life for a freer, more self-determined one. Many young girls became sisters filled with illusions of helping to shape a better world. They saw the congregations, despite their exaggerated restrictions and rules, as places where a spirit of selflessness might be developed, where real service could be given.

As these women advanced in their capacity for political (and personal) analysis, the orders began to feel too confining. They needed to break away. But they were loathe to give up the community, the collective support they had enjoyed. Feminist community often made the transition less jolting. Later, feminist analysis and practice enabled women to evolve new, more gynocentric forms of ritual, more in keeping with the relationships they wished to nurture among themselves and with the earth, their ideas, and other human beings.

Other feminists, although they may also be part of a deeply Christian tradition (broadly imposed by the European conquest of the Americas), came to their gender consciousness by way of a Left political involvement. These are often university-educated women who participated in the Marxist and/or Maoist student movements of the 1960s and '70s. Or they are women from the factories and farms whose very conditions of life make worker equality appealing.

Latin America's New Left (Cuba's 26th of July Movement, the Sandinistas in Nicaragua, Uruguay's Tupamaros, the Chilean MIR, guerrilla movements in Argentina, El Salvador, Bolivia, Brazil) articulated a gender difference with the older Communist party configurations: they took endemic sexism into account. No longer did they claim that class struggle and economic independence alone would bring equality between the sexes.

The rhetoric varied and in some cases promised qualitative change. Gender analyses were put forward, though they rarely informed political strategies in ways that challenged patriarchal values or control. Some revolutionary organizations instituted quotas by which a third or even half of the mid-level leadership had to be female. The FMLN in El Salvador was a leader in this respect. Since the making of this book, the Sandinistas in Nicaragua have instituted a one-third quota for women in leadership.

Throughout the tumultuous 1970s women fought and died alongside their men; they talked about prolonged battle situations being the surest remedy against a reversion to the old ways. "Men don't mess with women with guns" became a popular slogan as the last decades of the century got underway. But a troubling backlash was also beginning to be apparent. Once situations of extreme crisis gave way to whatever version of pseudo-peace, men expected women to retreat to their traditional roles. And many women retreated. Socially (and economically) they had little choice. The male power structures had essentially remained intact.

During periods of intense social change, those women who managed most easily to shape their ideas and expectations to the male model were those who moved into positions of relative influence. Of course that influence—at least insofar as a feminist vision is concerned—was greatly circumscribed by this fact. The women had gotten where they were because the men permitted their ascent. The men permitted their ascent because they didn't see them as a serious threat.

When the socialist experiments began to unravel, when the new Latin American social projects began to be defeated (by U.S. strategies of conquest and local disarticulation and corruption), old forms of domination and control began to reassert themselves. People's governments went under. Investment capital appeared on the scene to nurture free market economies and strengthen unequal power relations. Individual "freedoms" replaced collective gain. Women and racial or ethnic minorities were once again relegated to an inferior position. Unique among the affected groups, however, women seemed to survive this betrayal.

Perhaps the *sort* of understanding brought about by feminist analysis helped women (and our male allies) to see more clearly where our efforts had veered off course. I believe that women's retrieval of memory is central here. The ability to reconnect with a damaged Self, to *re-member* what was done to us and by whom, to understand how abuse determined our subsequent sense of identity, has made it possible for us to survive. The fact that society protects the perpetrators is one more reason to change society.

We have redesigned language, and this new way of speaking serves as a constant reminder of who we are and what we want. In many places we have reclaimed the female pronoun when talking about a woman. In a more thoroughly gendered language such as Spanish, it's much more than the pronoun that's changed. And we have also begun to name persons and events more accurately: not "I was raped," but "Someone (a proper name, if known) raped me." Not the passive construction which treats events as if they simply occur, but the assignment of responsibility in how we speak. Intentionality. Choice.

In that border territory between English-speaking Belize and Nicaragua's Caribbean Coast, other women's realities emerge. Debbie Ewens tells the story of a life formed in a confluence of worlds. Mayan, African, Scottish, Spanish, Chinese, and English blood are her heritage. Debbie's great-grandmother was a midwife in Bluefields; for years she kept a black book with the names and birth dates of everyone she helped bring into the world. She lived to be 106. We know too little about women in Belize, even less about their creole, mixed-blood, and Indian sisters from the several tribes that inhabit the Nicaraguan side of an arbitrary border.

Ewens brings us new questions, different patterns of speech, another flavor to the term feminist. Still, there are recognizable echoes: the scorned ancestry of racism, the pride of heritage surviving through generations of women, a resistance to accepting the colonizer's language and assumptions. Belize isn't present on the tourist posters or in our news media. Its name doesn't even demand our attention at most of the international conferences. I was delighted at the very last moment to be able to include the voice of a woman whose people remain so distant from our lives.

Magaly Pineda's story traces one person's history—and through hers, the history of a movement. We listen to a woman who was born into an upwardly mobile family in the Dominican Republic, an island nation long controlled by U.S. interests. Magaly's father wanted a boy; for a month after her birth he routinely opened her diaper and exclaimed "Impossible!" when confronted with her female genitalia. Magaly's mother possessed an entrepreneurial creativity and strength that allowed her to overcome severe depression, develop the business skills necessary to support her family, and eventually free herself from the oppression of a philandering husband.

Magaly moved from the typical convent school (and her childhood desire to become a nun) to the larger world of literature and philosophy; and then into her country's underground revolutionary movement. Married to a man who spent years in prison for his ideas and more recently won a national congressional seat, she founded an alternative school and then one of the most important centers for research on women and feminist activism on the continent. CIPAF,[1] as it is called, has a fifteen-year history and has become a moving force in Dominican life. It's been important as well to feminists in other Latin American countries. Magaly talks about her own life and feminism in her country, moving back and forth in a story where all the issues connect.

The conversation with lesbians in Nicaragua took place in the fall of 1991. A lesbian, gay, and bisexual movement there had emerged as early as 1985, about halfway through the Sandinista decade. While the Nicaraguan revolution managed to avoid the repressive measures which in Cuba it is taking so long to overcome, organizing wasn't to be completely smooth. Certain FSLN leaders understood the issue of gay rights, others were less enthusiastic. Nicaragua's lesbian, gay, and bisexual movement has its own history of repression, silencing, and fear.

The women who spoke with me through that long night in Managua were from Europe and the United States as well as from Nicaragua. Such bridges are common in this book. Their stories of how they came to terms with their own sexuality, how they found one another, and how their movement evolved, trace a compelling history of dignity and commitment. Different women remember differently and this adds to the richness of the conversation.

For a North American reader it is interesting that Nicaraguan lesbians, gays, and bisexuals see their issues as part of the overall struggle for social change, part of their revolutionary project. They believe that as an oppressed group they deserve the freedom and respect due workers, farmers, women, and the indigenous communities of the Atlantic Coast.

It is worth noting that this claim to freedom of sexual identity is being made in a deeply Catholic country, where chaperons were common in the not too distant past and even such mildly "deviant" behavior as premarital heterosexual relations are frowned upon among all but the poorest sectors of society (where such requirements are overlooked because people don't have the money, not because they believe them unnecessary). On the other hand, Nicaragua—like most of the Latin world—has an entrenched double standard for men. Married men have long lived by a set of rules that accepts *la casa chica*[2] as a matter of course.

During the Sandinista war against the dictatorship and the decade of people's government that followed, the sexual double standard was addressed in a variety of forums—at least as regards heterosexual conduct. Within the party, struggles were waged by women who demanded they be judged by the same standards as their brothers. The fact that the Nicaraguan revolution came to power in 1979, when feminism had become an international concern, made it much easier to address these issues than it had been in Cuba (where much of the revolutionary leadership remained limited by a pre-1959 mentality).

But recognition of homophobia and an acceptance of homosexuality were further bridges to be crossed. Nicaraguan lesbians, especially, have been at the forefront of this struggle. They have also broken ground with analyses that link homophobia and heterosexism to other social ills. In a few short years the gay community has initiated its own celebration of Gay Pride, organized a formal presence on revolutionary holidays, hosted public educational forums for the press and general public, promoted non-sexist sex education, and structured comprehensive AIDS outreach and advocacy.

The next piece, about a magical visit to the General Cemetery in Santiago de Chile, might seem as if it doesn't belong. It has nothing to do with Central America or the Caribbean. It isn't even (primarily) about women. Its inclusion is important to me precisely because it evokes my own connection to Latin America: as a woman, as a person permanently displaced in all these worlds, and as someone who has shared the drama of exile, chosen or imposed.

My youngest daughter was in Santiago doing her junior year abroad. I visited her there in November, 1993. Aside from my eagerness to see Ana, the trip was a homecoming of a different kind. I had been in Chile in 1972, during the Allende years.[3] In October there was a truck-owners' strike and martial law was declared. I remembered sleeping wherever the 11 p.m. curfew caught me as I tried to get to know a country that was living through a kind of dress rehearsal for the terror to come.

In that autumn of 1972, and in spite of ominous portents, Santiago was still energized by a dream. I visited shanty towns where neighbors had organized healthcare and schools. City walls were bright with murals. People talked about *their* copper, *their* future. Then, less than a year later, came the coup.

What many of us knew back then is accepted history now. The CIA, aided by local interests, staged the bloodiest takeover in contemporary Latin American history. No one will ever know exactly how many were murdered; 70,000 was one number projected at the time. Sports stadiums were turned into prisons. Bodies backed up in morgues and in the waters of the Mopocho River. Seventeen years of ferocious dictatorship followed, and Milton Freidman and his Chicago School were charged with designing a model of economic success in the southern cone.

Some of the people I had known in Chile became a part of the great diaspora that spread across the continent and beyond. Some I would never hear from again; they simply disappeared, swallowed up in the terror. And, in the magic-realist manner so indigenous to Latin America, a few women and men who had been prominent in the Allende government somehow survived that long winter of repression and returned to old battlegrounds of political struggle.

Such was the case of Mireya Baltra. She had been a member of Allende's cabinet in the early 1970s, survived the coup and those hard years of exile, and now was back campaigning for senator on the Communist ticket. A strong symbol of continuity if ever there was one. As we drove through Isla Negra on our way to visit Pablo Neruda's museum home I noticed her name painted on the coastal cliffs.

My last day in Santiago, Ana, her partner Louis, and I were still enjoying the freedom of a rental car. We had a couple of extra hours and suddenly found ourselves in the general cemetery: where they'd brought the bodies twenty years before. *"Gracias a la vida"* is about those two hours, what we saw and heard, what happened—in this dimension and in that other reality hovering just beyond our reach. *"Gracias a la vida"* is as much about my own relationship to Latin America as anything I've written.

The last piece in this collection is a series of vignettes reflecting my observations and experiences on two separate visits to Cuba: in April-May and in December of 1993. I lived and raised my four children in Cuba from 1969 through the end of 1980. In many ways those were the glory years of the Cuban revolution. Much has happened since, in my own life as well as in the history of this single remaining socialist experiment in the Americas.

The long and short of it is that the revolution has survived. Aware of the orchestrated effort (now 35 years old) that has tried to destroy the Cuban project, I always come away from Cuba marvelling that the revolution is still alive rather than bemoaning its many obvious problems.

These 1990s trips were feminist excursions, organized for the purpose of giving North American women the opportunity of speaking with women in Cuba. We visited women on construction crews and members of parliament. We went to maternity hospitals and explored the articulation of a lesbian community. We conversed with women artists and writers and went to factories where most of the labor force was female. As happens among women, we heard lots of stories.

I wanted to close this collection with my Cuban piece precisely because I feel strongly that this is where the hope resides: in a revolution that has had its problems, internal as well as from without, that has perhaps been slow to embrace certain premises that we as feminists hold dear, but that has managed against all obstacles to hold onto its project of social equality. Today the Cuban revolution is opening to ideas it once found too difficult to address: such as the right of religious believers to policy-making positions, or lesbian and gay identity as worthy of respect.

Women in Cuba have traveled a difficult road. Their participation in the anti-dictatorship struggle earned them a place in reconstruction. The international as well as the domestic economic situation in 1959 opened numerous avenues for advancement—and for independence. On the one hand, feminism as an ideological component was not really on the agenda back then. On the other hand, the Cuban Communist Party was influenced by, even as it sometimes veered away from, the more traditional communist concepts of women in society.

In Cuba's efforts to build its own brand of socialism women quickly acquired educational levels previously reserved for men. They entered new professions and excelled. The Federation of Cuban Women, a grass-roots organization which now includes 80% of the female population fourteen years and older, has done a good job of channelling women's energies in defense of the revolution. It has been less successful in its ability to look deeply at gender-specific issues.

My personal experience during the many years I lived in Cuba taught me that openness and rigidity followed a rather predictable curve: when hostility from the United States would intensify, when the Cubans felt most acutely the pressure of forces bent on their destruction, they tended to pull in, to assume a more defensive position in which criticism was frowned upon and unity preserved at almost any cost. When things got better, when the tensions relaxed to whatever extent, inevitably there would be a gesture towards expansion. Discussion of difficult questions was then encouraged, creativity surfaced in more complex ways, tolerance blossomed, individual difference was recognized and respected.

Perhaps what struck me most powerfully on these recent visits to Cuba was the apparent reversal of this equation. Clearly the revolution was having a very hard time. The disintegration of the Soviet Union and the rest of the European socialist bloc had left the country bereft of its most important trading partners. Indeed the whole economic and political system of which Cuba was a member had fallen apart. Meanwhile, the United States continued to intensify its many-pronged attack. Right-wing Cuban exile groups became more active. Nor was Cuba immune to the fallout from capitalism's own economic crisis, or to a series of natural disasters that battered the island in the early 1990s. Nevertheless, in the midst of this very palpable hardship I found Cubans more willing to discuss their errors, more encouraging of criticism, and more open to new ideas on each successive visit.

This stunned me. And I think it is a product of authentic revolution. Old friends rode heavy Chinese or Russian bicycles to work, because there was no gasoline. People were thinner than I'd ever seen them, and hunger was a frequent topic of conversation. Some believed Fidel Castro had been in office too long; others didn't see how anyone but he could extricate them from the current crisis. Still, the major social programs—education, daycare, universal healthcare—were working. Yes, there were problems (such as hospital patients having to provide their own sheets and sometimes even to bring a light bulb from home), but the programs themselves were intact. In Cuba people still mean more than profit.

These have been particularly interesting times in which to speak with women in Cuba. Obviously, some of the long-won gains are beginning to erode; and women are often the ones who feel this most acutely. For example, when vegetable oil and laundry soap are in dramatically short supply, women are reluctant to leave the cooking or laundry to men who may be wasteful in their inexperience.

Women with whom we spoke disagreed about the effects of the special period[4] on their lives. Some felt it was setting them back, pushing them to accept situations of discrimination they had believed to be a thing of the past. Shortages of raw materials have slowed or shut down certain factories; many women (and also men) have been sent home with 60% of their salaries. For women this often means a reversal to more traditional household responsibilities. Other women, though, believe that the current crisis—which has put all Cubans on the line—has actually moved them forward in some undefined way. I could sense what they meant. Up-against-the-wire drama often brings people together around issues central to their humanity. There's less time or inclination for pretense; or for the excuses that so often act as a brake on social progress.

I have spoken about the ways in which feminists throughout Latin America have developed: some emerging from the ranks of the communist and socialist movements or out of the New Left; others coming up through the Christian movement that exploded after Vatican II. Feminist movements in other places, especially the United States and Europe, have also had an influence. Today respectful and energizing relations exist between feminists of different persuasions, and the influence moves in both directions.

Latin American feminists are also retrieving historic models of creativity and strength. Often the myths must be reexamined and corrected in order to free them of patriarchal distortion. This is clear in both the piece on Guatemalan women and the interview with Belize's Debbie Ewens.

One such myth with importance for all Latin Americans is the story of *La malinche*. She was an Indian woman whose parents sold her into slavery and who was presented at the age of 15 to Hernán Cortés, the Spanish conqueror of ancient Mexico. She was his translator, into Mayan as well as Nahuatl. *La malinche* was passed from officer to officer as a sexual favor, bore a child to one of them, and died in her early twenties after a lifetime of abuse.

In traditional Latin American lore, *La malinche* has come to represent the traitor, the woman who betrayed her race by going with and bearing a child to the European invader. It may be indicative of many such myths that the blame is laid upon the victim—the young girl sold against her will—rather than upon the real perpetrator: the white male European *conquistador*. In modern-day Spanish, *malinchismo* has become a noun, denoting an act of betrayal.

Latin American feminists are revising this history and retrieving the real meaning of this woman's life. Today *La malinche* speaks of race (the mixed race which belongs to most of the continent's inhabitants) and gender in a reexamined history of rape and survival. I first heard the revision of the *La malinche* myth from a feminist in Managua.

Perhaps because of its particular history of revolution, Nicaragua is the place where the most powerful feminist movement seems to be consolidating itself—theoretically as well as in its multifaceted activism. And I'd like to end this introduction with a more recent story from Nicaragua. It concerns Vidaluz Meneses: poet, head of that country's library system for most of the Sandinista administration, now Dean of Arts and Letters at Managua's Jesuit University. The story is about how Vidaluz got the position she now holds.

The president of the University approached her one day and offered her the post. But Vidaluz didn't accept, not right away. Instead she said she'd have to think about it and would get back to him in a week or so. When a couple of weeks had passed and he'd heard nothing, the University president called her again. "I'll give you my answer in a few days," Vidaluz said. "I'm attending a conference this weekend where a number of other women will be, and I want to confer with them."

The following Monday, Vidaluz finally responded to the president's offer: "I've been talking it over with other women on campus," she told him, "and I've found at least three who could do the job as well as I. The four of us feel fine about it being given to any one of us. But whoever you choose, the other three must be named her top-ranking advisors, so we can work closely together."

This is how Vidaluz insisted upon a team of strong and talented women, not simply a token appointment. The president agreed, and these four women comrades are now reorganizing the school. There's no doubt in my mind that this speaks of women seeing themselves qualitatively differently with regard to their social role.

Notes

1. *Centro de Investigación Para la Acción Femenina* (Research Center for Women's Action).
2. Other households in addition to the official one.
3. 1970-73, when Salvador Allende's Popular Unity enjoyed a brief three years in office. His coalition of progressive parties was the first democratically elected socialist government in the Americas.
4. Fidel Castro has called this emergency in peacetime a "special period."

Chichicastenango

Santa Cruz del Quiché

Santa Cruz del Quiché

Santa Cruz del Quiché

Santa Cruz del Quiché

Chichicastenango

Santa Cruz del Quiché

Women carry immense baskets of produce, Guatemala City.

Chichicastenango

1

Invasion and Resistance
Guatemalan Women Speak[1]

✳

Guatemala, 42,042 square miles. Third largest country in Central America (roughly the size of Kentucky). Population 8.6 million, about 65% of whom are Mayan Indians. Basic exports: coffee, cotton, sugar, beef, cardamom, bananas, oil, and all the sesame seeds for McDonald's Big Mac buns. Spanish is the official language, although there are 22 Indian languages with more than 120 dialects. Life expectancy is 63 years, though it is much less for Indians than for Ladinos. The mortality rate for children under 5 is 103 per 1,000 live births (1987). Sixty-five percent of the population lacks health services. Only 45% of the adult population can read (compared to 77.4% in the rest of Central America). Five percent of Guatemalans receive 60% of the national income. The poorest 50% receive 7%. More than three-quarters of the population lives below the poverty line. With the most unequal land distribution in all of Latin America, 61.8% of arable land is owned by 4.28% of the landowners. Eighty-five percent of rural households are landless. Among many violator nations, Guatemala has the hemisphere's worst record for human rights. Between 1966 and 1986, more than 100,000 civilians were murdered and 38,000 people were *disappeared*, notably by Guatemalan military and paramilitary groups. Between 1978 and 1983, the army razed 440 rural villages. Even the country's own government sources estimate 100,000 children orphaned by political violence in the early 1980s.

I lean over the developing tray, agitating the print with bamboo tongs. Slowly, under the yellow glow of my darkroom safe light, two figures darken on the paper. A woman, her back to me, walks towards the door of a church off-camera to the right. I snapped the shutter so I know that the church door is there, although those who view this image may not see it. Behind the woman walks a girl child, a miniature replica of her mother.

The brilliance and density of the picture are almost perfect now. Although this is black-and-white photography, the exuberant colors return through recent memory. Deep wine red, brown, pale yellow, purple, rich green, startling pink. Color is a part of what this black-and-white picture is about. What these lives are about. Yet I know I prefer the starkness of intimation, none of the answers given.

As I lift the print from the tray, holding it up to let the excess chemical drip away, I think this child is not a child. By her size I might judge her five, maybe six years old. By her stance and gesture she is but a smaller version of the older woman she follows. The child-woman's face is not altogether turned away from the camera's eye. The set of her mouth, her intention, is clearly defined.

Mother and daughter are wearing the wrap-around hand-woven *corte* of the Guatemalan highlands. Their heavily embroidered *huipiles* are tucked into the skirt's waist beneath a woven sash which is wound and fastened beneath itself. Were I more familiar with the meaning of pattern, style, color, they would tell me the region, the exact village, and other details of these women's lives.

Double braids hang long down both strong backs; the mother's, plaited with ribbons, end in a bow just above her hips. Mother and daughter wear Western shoes: imitation leather with low heels. Twenty or thirty years ago (I am guessing) they would have walked barefoot, the calluses of their feet alone carrying them through these streets.

I move the print through a stop solution and into the tray of fix. Then I set the tongs on the counter and rest my chin in my hands. I want to look at this image for a while. There is something about the child's step. I look at her ankle and flexed foot, already old. Discarded corn husks are scattered on the stone steps and both mother and child are trampling them as if they are not there. But how can I ascribe unconsciousness or consciousness to this mother, this daughter? On a ledge built into the church wall is something that looks like crumpled paper. In my eyes it resembles a sea shell, one of those big ones you can hold to your ear and hear the surge of a distant tide.

I will repeat this pondering, questioning, dreaming assessment of each picture as I move one after another from tray to tray and their facsimiles return me to the market at Chichicastenango, a bus ride into Chimaltenango, the streets of Cobán, the broad central plaza in Guatemala City. Pictures of women. Pictures of women with whom I share this condition of mother, daughter, lover, worker. Pictures of women so different from myself that I discard one combination of words after another in my effort to bring their living to life upon the page.

This is about women at the margin and at center. What is margin and center with regard to who we are, where we live, inside as well as outside ourselves? And who suggests the label? Why even speak of labels? Because our living is so essentially about how we are viewed and how we view who we are in the world.

They aren't as sophisticated as we. How often have we heard this or a similar comment made about people different from ourselves? The statement implies more than a definition of sophistication. It emanates from an egocentric (often also ethnocentric, eurocentric, androcentric, and ruling class) focus which nowhere questions *we* as center. Consequently everyone, everything else, is margin. Other.

This is about Guatemalan women, most of them Indian, some Ladina (of mixed Indian and Spanish blood). Some speak Spanish as a second or third language, others tell their stories in Quiché or Kekchi or Mam. These women remember their Mayan ancestors, a complex culture out of which the concept of zero first entered our compendium of knowledge.

Today—and it's been a very long today—painful poverty, terror, and loss are central facts of these women's lives. In whatever their language, words like *torture, disappearance, strategic hamlet, hunger* have become stalwarts of their vocabulary. The *feelings* such conditions engender are expressed by words and in hard-to-translate silence.

And this is about ten women from the United States. Most of us had never met before coming together for this trip. One more margin/center dichotomy: whatever our circumstances, we *are* able to travel, visit, set the terms of these encounters. Few of the Guatemalan women with whom we meet can conceive of the idea of coming to where we live.

During the month of August, 1990 ten North American women from diverse backgrounds spent time with women in Guatemala. We came together under the sponsorship of the Washington-based Guatemala Health Rights Support Project, a Non Governmental Organization (NGO) that channels funding to community projects in that country as well as carrying out educational work in the United States. The criteria about who would participate, who we would speak to when we got there, and what kind of information we would share, responded to a feminist—and essentially new—conception of what might constitute a positive experience for women here and there.

Gretchen Noll of the Project, and Marie Moore—a Maryknoll Sister whose work for the past twenty years has been with Guatemalan women (often in exile)—wanted to experiment with a different type of visit. They no longer believed that the standard fact-finding mission was the most useful—where presumed experts arrive, ask questions, fill notebooks with their answers, and leave. Women, Gretchen and Marie knew, are able to talk to one another. Even women as obviously foreign to each other's way of life as feminists from the United States and Indian women in Guatemala would be able to share our stories.

So these were some of the key ideas: an active interest in popular struggle in Guatemala and a frustration at our government's role in perpetuating a terrorist state in that country, a feminist consciousness regarding the ways in which we wanted to approach our visit, the sense that we have something to give as well as much to learn, and a respect for women's stories—our collective memory. We would travel and meet with women in different areas of resistance. We would use public transportation wherever possible. And we would bring our own lives in offering.

We were a biologist, a geriatrics nurse, a resort manager, a religious sister, a woman who works in a battered women's shelter, a writer, and a woman who works for one of the leading African-American women's health projects, among others. We were Seneca, Mohawk, Chicana, African-American, and Jewish. We were lesbian and heterosexual women (about evenly divided). We ranged in age from 73 to 30. Our areas of work and activism differed broadly and we each had our reasons for wanting to make this trip at this particular time. Half of us were mothers and some of us grandmothers.

I lived most of my adult life in Latin America, first in Mexico, then in Cuba, and finally in Nicaragua. For me this trip was my first journey back to Central America since I'd won my five-year battle with the U.S. Immigration and Naturalization Service.[2] While under threat of deportation I had not been able to travel and I would learn just how much anticipation, fear, and gratitude the experience engendered. Poet, photographer, teacher, I'd spent years collecting the oral histories of women in places like Guatemala.

Places like Guatemala but not Guatemala itself. Before this trip I had never been inside that country. Still it wasn't entirely unknown to me; its history and mine had touched in deeply powerful ways. In 1969 I had translated a book called *Let's Go!* by Otto-Rene Castillo. Two years earlier, this important revolutionary poet and a woman comrade named Nora País had been captured and burned alive by their country's repressive forces. They were members of the revolutionary movement which is still engaged in active struggle there and which today, in the coalition called URNG (Guatemalan National Revolutionary

37

Unity), is involved in ongoing though currently stalemated talks with the Guatemalan government.

As our visit unfolded, the lines of Otto-Rene's verse would sometimes whisper in my head: "*Vámonos patria a caminar, yo te acompaño.* Let's go, country, I will go with you. / I will descend the depths you claim for me. / I will drink of your bitter chalices. / I will remain blind that you may see…." Throughout my years in Latin America I had known many Guatemalans who had figuratively or literally chosen blindness so their country might see; many had given their lives to that effort, others are still committed to it. On this journey I was always conscious of feeling a closeness to their history. A people descended from the Mayans: inheritors of their richness of science and spirituality, struggling against enormous odds to reap the benefits of the society their culture has helped to shape.

So I was eager to travel with North American women to speak and listen to women in Guatemala. The opportunity seemed ready made. We were urged to take only what we could easily carry. I packed light in every area but film; I toted 60 rolls and happily anticipated shooting most of it. And I knew I would be translating for the group. Only two of the other women spoke Spanish fluently although about half had some knowledge of the language. Language, memory, place: these are cultural foci to which I too feel particularly connected—and with increasing consciousness in recent years. My immigration battle had placed my own speech and landscape in painful jeopardy. A recent struggle to decipher a history of childhood sexual abuse also engaged, for me, the centrality of memory. Preparing to travel to Guatemala I found myself thinking of the importance of language in a country where the official tongue is the conqueror's. I thought about women's re-membering, how it feeds generations. I knew how precious place must be for a people suffering decades of forced disappearance, displacement, exile.

Our group assembles as one after another of our flights land at the vast Mexico City airport. Our contact with the Guatemalan diaspora is immediate. Marie has worked since its inception with something called *El comité del DF* (the Capital City Committee), a group of Guatemalans living and working in this metropolis of more than twenty million. One of the Committee's projects is a mental health workshop where exiles can deal with issues of displacement, torture, solidarity, cultural difference, possible guilt at having left, poverty, and the political situation back home.

Our first afternoon as a group we spend with three women from the workshop. I will call them Margarita, Isabel, and Concepcion. They have been outside Guatemala for eight years, forced to flee with their husbands during the intensification of political repression in the early 1980s. One had children when she arrived, the other two have become mothers during these Mexican years. Alice Walker has pointed out that most of the indigenous people in the world today are refugees, have been refugees, or are about to become refugees. I think about this, conscious of the fact that these women, not I, represent the norm.

Our conversation with the women in Mexico covers many aspects of their situation, then pinpoints the problems inherent in choosing to organize in women-only groups. "It's not easy," Margarita says. "We have our own problems, but when we take a feminist stance the men accuse us of being divisive...." We listen to this woman from the highlands of Guatemala, a Quiché Indian woman in exile. The issue is familiar to us all. A member of our group responds by saying yes, we've heard the old argument: if you're a feminist you must be a lesbian. I had not expected so soon to have to decide whether or where to be out. But I cannot be silent.

"We can't let the enemy define our terms," I begin, wondering how to phrase what I am about to say. "I am a feminist. And I am also a lesbian." And I talk about the need to address all forms of discrimination. Margarita, older and perhaps more experienced at these encounters than the other women, evidences no surprise. But Concepcion doesn't let the opportunity pass: "Wait," she says. "My friends and I...we discuss things, but I've never met a lesbian before, I mean not someone willing to talk...."

And so we talk. A couple of the others in our group come out as well, including the woman who had originally linked feminism and lesbianism. The Guatemalan women want to spend more time with us when we come back. For the North Americans this journey has begun with powerful energy. Our feminist practice of speaking to one another as women, of sharing our lives and issues as we listen to theirs, promises an experience that will surely go deeper than the fact-finding mission we are already working hard to avoid.

Our arrival in Guatemala City brings us up against a state of colloquial violence that pervades earth, air, people's eyes. A tourist may come and go and never see it. This is clear to me much later when, meeting a friend for tea at one of the elegant hotels in Zone Ten, I watch families with matched luggage and surf boards roam the lobby. But now we emerge from a couple of hours' flying over land that holds the ruins of Tikal, the secrets of a civilization that resists centuries of rape—genocide in all its forms. Expectant, we make our way through immigration and customs and out into the light of early afternoon.

The taxis that take us towards our modest hotel stop and start up again in a tangle of buses, jeeps, private cars. This is no ordinary traffic jam. It's a demonstration. Crowds of people on foot join those who are riding in shouted campaign chants and raised Vs for victory. It is a mammoth show of support for the candidacy of Efraín Ríos Montt, a general who was president during one of the country's worst periods of violence. Elections are in five months. Guatemala's constitution prohibits an ex-president from running again, but these demonstrators don't look like they'll take no for an answer.

This show of support depresses me. Ríos Montt is a hardcore member of the Church of the Word, one of several fundamentalist sects that now claim some 30% of Guatemala's population. These are people who were once solidly Catholic and earlier Mayan. Later some will give us higher figures—40 or 50% are now embracing protestantism, they say. As is true elsewhere in the world, here religious fundamentalism spearheads the far right's repressive thrust. The General puts forth a rabid "law and order" line. And it seems that even many of the peasants and working poor who suffered most during his first regime have been won over by vague promises of an end to corruption, misery, and fear.

Political violence and the violence of ordinary crime seem to mesh across the face of this exuberant landscape. Not unlike the pollution and grime superimposed upon what must once have been a beautiful colonial city. Guate, people call it for short. After settling briefly in our hotel we decide to take a city bus to a street fair in one of the poorer neighborhoods. It's our first experience of life here: the smells of roast corn and herbs, children laughing and screeching as the ferris wheel goes round, families and couples—many of them in traditional dress—wandering among the attractions.

Returning to our lodging we talk about these first sights of indigenous culture, our expectations and feelings. Suddenly Beth realizes she is missing her money and a pair of prescription sunglasses, all that she had in a small pack clasped about her waist. In the crush of the bus, deft fingers unzipped the pack, removed its contents, even zipped it up again. We had been warned that the desperation of life here makes this common. But we hadn't expected it on our first day.

Then Lisa notices that a cloth shoulder bag worn inside her jeans jacket has been slit its length. Some of what it held has also been taken. Within an hour: two thefts. One more clue to understanding what has been done to a nation of people who once lived in spiritual and communal harmony.

On tired wooden benches and folding chairs that could easily jackknife for the last time today beneath the weight of some of us, thirteen women sit in a loose circle within the space—dirt floor, three walls, tin roof—that serves as a Presbyterian Church. "*La Invasion*, The Invasion…." Margarita pauses and leans into the circle, repeating these words we hear no matter where we go.

By now we know that she is not talking about 1944 or '54, when the CIA backed invasions against the only democratically elected governments in this country's modern history. Neither is she remembering the scorched earth and strategic hamlet invasions of the early '80s, high points of terror in the contemporary repression that has claimed the existence of 442 rural villages and 38,000 people *disappeared*[3] (almost half of those in all of Latin America).

We have been in Guatemala nearly a week. We know, because we have heard it from the lips of women of several ethnicities and in as many differing situations, that *La Invasión*— spoken like that, with the emphasis of capital letters—refers to 1492. Margarita knows we are on a mission of solidarity and she hopes to bridge some part of the distance between us by telling this story about other women of similar intent: visitors from Spain who recently sat on these same benches, in this same electric space:

"They were talking about returning," she says, "reenacting Columbus's voyage after 500 years." She rocks on her spindly seat. Her voice grows hoarse with emotion. "A celebration, or maybe a commemoration of some kind…they even mentioned the sailing vessels: three ships modeled after the Nina, the Pinta, and the Santa María. And this woman asked me what I thought about the anniversary of the Conquest. I was silent."

Margarita's smile, like the reverse impression of a photographic negative, is dull where it should have been bright, curved down where it might have lifted. She looks from one to another of us and repeats: "I was silent. I didn't speak and so she asked me again: what do you think? Finally I told her: I am not going to be able to be gracious about your commemoration, because for us it is not something we feel like celebrating. For us these five hundred years have brought us nothing but abuse, rape, genocide. The death of our cultures. Please understand, I cannot become excited about your reenactment."

We too are silent, each immersed in our particular memories of what Columbus Day evokes. In our country of course the day is named for the man who led the expedition. The official quincentennial celebration with all its lies and bombast is already taking shape. Throughout Latin America October 12 is *El día de la raza*, Day of the Race. Which race is a question people are beginning to ask.

But Margarita's story isn't over. "The Spanish woman was quiet for a few moments," she continues, "and then she spoke: I want to ask you to forgive us, she implored. But I told her that one woman asking for forgiveness is not enough. Not enough for all we have suffered. Later we found out that one of the sailing ships had been burned," Margarita's smile almost turns positive image, "I think the Spanish solidarity committee may have been responsible...."

Josefina's small hands barely touch across her lap. Her fingers occasionally smooth the complex weave that is her *corte*, three yards of dark fabric wound and wrapped about her lower body. Like so many Guatemalan Indian women we have met she speaks of her *traje* with words that let us know it is essential to who she is. The *corte* and particularly the *huipil*, richly embroidered over-blouse, define region and village of origin as well as civil status and other identifying information. Two hundred and fifty different *trajes* are worn throughout this country.

We are sitting around a table in the house that serves as headquarters to CONFREGUA, an ecumenical grouping of the church sector. With us are women who work through the Christian Base Communities and with Protestant organizations. Increasingly these women are involved in programs that address consciousness raising, popular mobilization, and the struggle for the fulfillment of basic social needs. The conversation moves to include the women's richly embroidered dress.

"I was eight years old," Josefina says, "when my mother taught me how to weave the cloth. And then the embroidery."

Her syllables are soft and clipped in the even tones of the indigenous woman speaking her second language, which is Spanish. "I was allowed to choose the colors that would give me joy. My *traje* is a part of who I am."

The backstrap loom is the most common, although floor looms are used for larger lengths and widths of cloth. Everywhere we go women have come together in weaving collectives, sharing resources and skills to produce more and better fabric. But always the tradition is there, the art. It too is a part of the Guatemalan woman's identity. Many of the women are widows whose husbands have been murdered or disappeared during *The Violence*. Often young girls help with the embroidery.

In another part of the country, which I leave unnamed to protect the people with whom we speak, we spend an afternoon with a woman I will call Sara. The room in which she receives us is clearly hers: in one corner a small altar upon which the blessed corn and Christian cross share equal space, books and paintings and the faint fragrance of *copál* incense. A lone rooster crowing in the swatch of garden framed by wooden shutters occasionally punctuates our conversation. The sound is a welcome counterpoint to the incessant noise of large trucks or low-flying planes that conspire against us almost everywhere we go.

Sara traveled a part of the road towards becoming a priestess of her Mayan tradition but opted instead to practice nursing, the profession for which she studied in her provincial city. Recalling her years of schooling she provides further insights into the meaning of traditional dress in the lives of Guatemalan Indian women: "At the college there were only four of us who insisted upon wearing our *trajes*," she tells us. "The administration continued to try to get us to Westernize our dress the whole time we were there. But we resisted."

She speaks of the insidious racism still meted out to women who appear at government offices or other official institutions in the traditional dress that holds their memory of female identity. The scoffing, belittling attitudes that face a Quiché or Kekchi or Mam woman every time she comes in contact with this ongoing expression of invasion. And she speaks as well of her work in hospitals, of the valuable connection with indigenous patients her own *traje* has provided.

Sara works among her people, the Kekchi. She does community nursing and has been interested in systematizing the herbs, roots, and other plants cultivated for medicinal use by the old people, the wise. "They use them because they cost less," she explains, "and also because they tend not to produce the negative side effects of Western medicine." And she speaks of the rituals that accompany the gathering of plants: attention to the moon's cycle, prayers to ask forgiveness of the earth for having to pluck her produce.

This leads to a discussion of specific ills as well as of issues like menstruation and menopause and the attitudes the Indian women have towards these important changes in their lives. It is here that we stop to contemplate the fact that menstruation is a largely Western phenomenon, and a recent one. In these highlands—as in many other parts of the misnamed Third World— young women become pregnant with their first child coincident with or even before their first menses. Between successive pregnancies followed by long periods of nursing they live their years of fertility without bleeding every month. Menopause for these women, then, marks the end of childbearing rather than of menstruation.

Again I am struck by the marginality of my own experience when considering the lives of most of the world's women. Class, race, gender, and sexuality must be factored into analyses of commonality and difference. But so must culture—so central to how we live.

The meaning of traditional dress is made clear to us nowhere more vividly than in the presence of a tattered *corte* used by our group of U.S. women in empowering ritual. This piece of poor cloth, a rude mass of patched patches—blue, brown, a striped swatch of dirty white dotting the more prevalent red—has been reduced to little more than a yard from its original three. The Maryknoll Sister among us received this cast-off covering of a woman's body from another in her congregation and we carry it with us into the country and out. At different moments in our collective processing we spread it in our midst, taking strength from what we imagine to be the history of the woman to whom it belonged.

The story we learn is this. Sometime during the worst of the violence, 1982-86, a woman, one of thousands, was forced to flee a resistance village with her two small children. Through the mountainous highlands they made their way, struggling over an eight-year period until they reached one of the teeming refugee camps in southern Mexico. By that time her only cloth was reduced to the shambles we now use as amulet. A Maryknoll Sister at the camp provided her with a new *corte*, and so the old one passed from hand to hand until it came to rest among ten women from another world who would lose (or find?) ourselves in contemplation of its proud tenacious life. It is a visible, tangible expression of women's courage.

Such frequent manifestations of the importance of traditional dress for the Indian women of Guatemala lead us to questions about these women's feelings regarding those from outside appropriating their richly woven *huipiles*. Some of us have bought the embroidered tops at solidarity events or in the many U.S. outlets for indigenous apparel. I myself have worn the shifts from Mexico or Guatemala much of my life, drawn to their art of fabric, color, design. Now I am forced to question the legitimacy of my choice.

Gabina, one of the Presbyterian women in Chimaltenango, responds to our concern. "If she buys our clothing in order to help us live, if she wears it with respect for our way of life, then I feel good about seeing a woman from outside with one of my people's *huipiles*." She falls silent. Perhaps she has said as much as she wishes on the subject. But we press her further. What about the *corte*, we want to know. The women exchange looks of incredulity among themselves. It is clear that they have seen outsiders wearing their *huipiles* and have come to the conclusion just offered, either out of resigned expediency or from the heart. But another's use of the wrapped skirt is beyond their ability to conceive so generously of encroachment upon tradition. "No," Gabina says finally, "the *corte* no."

Identity is also and profoundly language. This is particularly important to people in a country where 22 separate indigenous tongues have yet to be given the same legal and institutionalized recognition as the invader's Spanish. The latter is official although native only to that 40% of the population called Ladino. All those others, although spoken by a much larger percentage of the population, remain different, other. To be so catalogued where you were born, where you live, where your parents and grandparents lived: it's a form of oppression shared by many in our world.

Many of us have read *I, Rigoberta Menchú*,[4] the extraordinary testimony of a Guatemalan Quiché Indian woman. Many in our own country have heard Rigoberta in person; since the political repression in her country forced her into exile, she works for the United Nations and tours frequently, speaking as eloquently as she writes of the torment of a people under constant threat of genocide. Language and the speaking of language are powerfully present in Rigoberta's tale. She spoke only her native Quiché until her conscious decision, at the age of 21, to learn Spanish "so as to be able to tell the story of my people."

I have taught *I, Rigoberta Menchú* at universities and colleges in the United States and each time I do I am newly impressed by this woman's decision: to learn a new language in order to be able to transmit a story which belongs not to an individual but to a people. A people who possess one of the richest cultures on earth, whose very survival resists an ongoing devastation that began five hundred years ago and has not ceased. But, as often happens with books, I had thought of Rigoberta's effort as unique until my own experience in Guatemala.

47

The scene is a modest colonial house in Zone Two, the central section of the capital city. Once a residence, the house has been leased for a year by CENTROCAP, an advocacy center through which two energetic women, Gloria and Eugenia, have been organizing women who work in private homes. This characterization—women who work in private homes—is one increasingly adopted by domestic servants coming together in several Latin American countries. Language being important, these women who represent one of the most exploited sectors of society will not call themselves servants, or the Spanish equivalents of washer woman, nanny, maid, chick, girl: or any of the indignities by which they are routinely taunted in our classist and racist societies.

We arrive to find the house teeming with women, many with small children (who are cared for in a makeshift converted garage). The adults are busy in different rooms. In Guatemala Indian women may begin to work as maids at the age of eight (who, then, is an adult?) and we see several women whose labor-lined faces signal they are in their sixties or older. Some study basic first aid, some read, others cut dressmaking patterns. But the shared experience grabs and holds us most profoundly when we gather in an open interior courtyard. Here, after brief formal introductions, one after another of these women who work in private homes steps forward eager to tell her story.

One, a slight woman dressed in a *traje* whose design I have not seen before, and with the calm reserve of her Indian culture, stands before us and begins: "I am a Mam woman," she says, "and Spanish is my second language. I will ask you to forgive my inability to speak as I would like; I learned Spanish when I came to work in the city and so that I could tell my story...." As one after another of these women tells us "I am Mam," "I am Quiché," I understand that Rigoberta Menchú is not alone in her fervent need to give voice to a story of terrible beauty and terrible oppression.

And the stories come fast in a kind of breathless rage: I came to the city as a child; I did not know what awaited me here.

My *patrón* (employer, man of the house) raped me; his sons think they have a right to my body. My *patrona* (mistress, woman of the house) did not believe me when I told her what was going on. They accused me of stealing money I didn't take and threw me out in the middle of the night; it was dark, I had nowhere to go. I have a small child. My *patrona* accused my baby girl of wetting the bed. She threw us out. It's hard to find work when you have children. My children are in my village; I haven't seen them in four months....

Women who live in the homes of their employers, who are on call 24 hours a day for an average $20-a-month salary, women who are lucky to get one day off out of fifteen and who enjoy no job security or benefits of any kind, have found a place where support and advocacy are forthcoming. As each speaks, her determined words encourage her sisters. They turn a meeting programmed for one hour into more than two of testimonial sharing.

We too speak of our lives and what we do. The indigenous women are particularly interested in what Beth and Loretta, our Mohawk and Seneca sisters, have to say. News of battered women's shelters touches a common nerve. Lisa, the African-American woman in our group, likens the stories she has heard to her own people's history of slavery: "The lucky ones were the house slaves," she says. Around the courtyard many of the Guatemalan women nod.

Gloria and Eugenia will not let themselves be coopted by the Guatemalan government agencies that opportunistically claim to address the needs of poor and working women. They have made their choice between official sponsorship and people's trust, and know they have come down on the side of danger. Both beg us to publicize the work they are doing "so that when the repression comes, and we know it will, we may be able to garner support from people on the outside." Eugenia adds that "We know we're not going to get any help from our own class; we're organizing the very women they treat as slaves."[5]

Alenka is an old friend, Chilean by birth, Guatemalan by virtue of marrying and raising her children in this place. A woman in her late forties. A poet. We first met ten years ago when I lived in Havana and she went there for medical help. Her oldest son had been found with his eyes gouged out a few blocks from their home, and she had lost her hearing as a result. His crime? Having belonged to a basketball team that played a game in Cuba. Later, Alenka and I lived for a period of time in Managua and our friendship consolidated itself there.

We were women approaching midlife, both of us poets, both living and working in revolutionary Nicaragua. Our children, four in each case, were close in age. Enough to bring us together. Now the Sandinistas have lost the election, we are older, and neither of us lives in Nicaragua anymore. Pieces of our souls remain in the streets of that country though. And we still make poems. Alenka sips her tea and asks me if I am living with someone: "*Tenés compañero?*, Do you have a lover?" "*Compañera*," I correct the gender. "I am with a woman." Wondering how she will take this news. "How wonderful," she responds, the old energy crinkling around her eyes. "Tell me about her," she urges.

When her mother grew ill Alenka returned to Guatemala City to care for her until her death. She's still here. We meet one afternoon for tea and to catch up on one another's lives. Divorced, living alone, managing an import-export firm, sometimes writing. She tells me she feels alone, lost in the morass of anguish and frustration she says this country has become. Few friends. No one to talk to.

This month marks the tenth anniversary of her son's death. José León was his name. Alenka confides, "We had a mass. That's all you can do here now: have a mass." We leave the sterile tea room and drive to the house once inhabited by a family: mother and father, daughters and sons. I remember that Roberto, Alenka's ex-husband, edited an important literary magazine at Guatemala's University of San Carlos. One editorial board after another was gunned down by paramilitary assassins and he barely got out alive. He went to Mexico just in time.

Now we enter the rooms of an empty house, the smell of stale air hitting us as we open each new door. Alenka shows me "where the kids and their friends sang and played guitars...the study where I wrote...in this corner of his room he had all his trophies." She is remembering her son. Across the street a mass of tin and cardboard shacks fills a long gully. On the far horizon the ever-present view of blue mountains, low clouds.

Alenka will sell this house and move away. With the money she hopes to live at least part of each year in Chile. "It's the only country in Latin America that has a viable project," she says. "It's not *my* project, but it's a project." She is talking about the centrist government that recently replaced 17 years of military dictatorship to the far south.

I can see that my friend is tired. She wants out of the violence, the unspeakable, the memories that surface in her dreams and in her poems. When she pulls her old Volkswagen station wagon alongside the curb by my hotel and gets out to hug me goodbye, I feel the ache of her body's curve. But also its irrepressible hope. In poets that's always the last to die.

We have come by intercity bus from the capital to Santa Cruz del Quiché. Through the vibrant countryside, every shade and hue of green. A patchwork of cultivated crops runs almost vertically up steep mountain slopes. Fast images of people walking by the side of the highway: carrying enormous loads, pushing or pulling animals of cargo, in small clusters, waiting. Often waiting. That kaleidoscope of impressions reserved for the traveler.

Late morning of our arrival we are marking time before our afternoon meeting with the women we have come to see. We lean, tired, on wooden tables in an open food stall at the edge of an empty amusement park. This is August 15, Feast of the Assumption of the Blessed Virgin, and the park is closed, perhaps for the parade. We have front row seats. Chicken and potatoes are being roasted over hot coals. The scent provokes our taste buds. Our plates are adorned as well with chopped onion and slices of full red tomatoes we have been warned not to eat. We pick at the food, eyes drawn to the pageant.

People line the street watching blocks of businessmen, students, religious and social societies, marching bands with their baton twirlers, women in traditional dress, all succeeding one another in the slow-moving ritual. I am startled by the incongruous strains of "Onward Christian Soldiers". The police in full dress uniform march with their bayonets bared. There is no festivity in people's eyes, neither the onlookers nor those taking part. Everyone seems slightly dulled, almost absent. An ominous helicopter dips low over the crowd.

After satisfying our bus hunger we walk through narrow streets to the Catholic Action house on the outskirts of town. There we are pulled into a large meeting room towards a central arrangement of beauty on the floor. A profusion of tiny white flowers covers a *metate* or stone for grinding corn. It stands upon a brightly woven cloth. One large candle is burning atop it all, and to the right also on the floor is a dish of *copál*, the pungent incense we smell so often where we go.

Several Quiché women rush forward to hold us in brief embrace. "Good afternoon, I am Lucía....Good afternoon, I am Xenia from (and the name of a village escapes my ears)....Welcome, I am Marta....Xionona....María...." Greetings, we will learn, which comprise the extent of these women's spoken Spanish. With them are Mary Anne and Judy, two Maryknoll Sisters from San Andrés Chiniqué. They have arranged this meeting and will translate for us all.

Arranging the meeting wasn't easy. Most of the women walked from villages one to two days' distant from San Andrés, spending their first night out at the sisters' house. The next day they all traveled together by jeep to Santa Cruz. The fifty miles between the two towns took four hours over the hard roads typical of those that web this highland country. After our meeting the women would reverse this procedure, spending another night with the sisters in San Andrés and then returning by foot to their mountain homes. Some will have been away from their families for five days in order to spend three or four hours with women from the United States they don't know and will not see again.

For women, that many days away from home and family also means leaving the cornmeal prepared for that many days of *tortillas*. It means arranging for children to be cared for or walking with them along mountain paths. Two of these women have infants on their backs. Another is accompanied by her son, perhaps eight or ten years old.

The sisters are among the first religious to return to this area after the severe repression of the early 1980s forced foreign church people out. They have been back in the area for five years now, waiting for the people to tell them what they need. So far, aside from elemental health work, they have undertaken a small orchard and a goat project. They have killed a goat for this occasion; we can smell it cooking along with boiled vegetables and fresh fruit in the kitchen across the courtyard.

Now we gather to share with these women. And it isn't easy. Their warm and open manner draws us in. Yet their lives have few if any points of convergence with our own. It's not a matter of unwillingness to speak, for each woman assumes her turn with energy; there is a rush of words, the gentle yet almost staccato sounds of the Quiché. Passion is clear in body language and their desire to make us understand.

Xionona nurses a two-year-old baby girl who looks no more than a year. The child was given to her by its natural mother who had twins and couldn't care for both. Since her own recent infant had died, Xionona's breasts were full. The twin boy was stronger, the girl "intended for death" as she explains. "But now she is healthy." She smiles down at the little girl, shifting her across her lap. "I gave her her name. She is mine," she says. The birth mother wants her back and Xionona aches at the thought of her impending loss.

María is a midwife. She responds to our questions about birthing practices in her community. And about how midwives acquire the skill, take up the task. One teaches another, of course; choosing your successor is important. One of the other women says she has always wanted to learn. They glance at one another, then consider the fact that they live several days' journey apart. I mention that I too have been a midwife. The women smile, experience creating a bridge between us.

Lucía tells us about her goats. She immediately begins to sob and her body shakes as she remembers. She had a wonderful female goat that gave birth to twins. And the twins were female too. "Yes, a promise of many future goats!" But her father one day decided she was not to keep the animals. Why, we ask? Too much trouble—or at least that is what we glean from the broken words as they make their way through Judy's translation from Quiché into Spanish, then mine from Spanish into English.

Why did her father hate the goats, we ask, why did he make her give them away? And again the explanation carries passion, words, sounds, silence, the tears that streak Lucía's face. Alcohol seems to be the answer. He drinks. And some of the women in our group begin to speak of alcoholism in our own communities, a common problem. Still, any complex understanding is spotty at best. Or is it? I feel a communication independent of words. Sometimes the sisters' attempts to simplify the dialogue make me nervous. Surely they know these women in ways we do not. Yet I wonder.

We talk about marriage; in this culture it is still decided for young girls by their parents. And about subsistence work, how it is organized. Among the women from the United States, those of us who can talk about protecting women and children from abuse, about health work, and about the importance of our individual stories are able to make connections that resonate on the faces of our Guatemalan sisters. Again translation is determined by Judy and Mary Anne, who know some Quiché.

When I want to share the fact that I have been persecuted because of my books—women's stories— Judy transmits this as "persecution for speaking out." The concept of a book, she says, is too far removed from these lives.

When we have exchanged our stories to the limits of what

we feel can be absorbed—on both sides—the women begin a ritual we have not previously observed. Mary Anne produces a handful of long thin tapers which she passes among us. We each light our individual candle from the large one burning on the *metate*. And then we follow the Indian women's lead in dripping wax on the floor and fixing the tapers around the centerpiece.

This is native to this part of the country, we are told; each woman fixes her candle as if she is planting herself in the earth, a way of honoring the hard work she has done throughout the preceding year. A celebration at the Feast of the Assumption: one of the many examples of the syncretism between Mayan and Christian traditions.

And then the women sing. Between verses of what are clearly religious hymns rendered in Quiché, they intone the Hail Marys and Our Fathers recognizable even in this other language. I am struck by the contrast between the rich art of their *trajes*, their headpieces, the ritual display they have so lovingly arranged for us, and the rote, almost numbing nature of this musical offering. One of the sisters tells me the hymns were translated by a local priest.

I cannot help but think of the infamous Summer Linguistic Institute operating in many of the developing nations, where supposed experts translate the New Testament into indigenous languages while gathering the most sensitive information about the groups whose terrain they invade. The Institute is active in Guatemala, I am told. And of course there are many more recent "institutes": the fundamentalist sects that have come in conquest of these peoples' land and lives.

We eat together, communicating with one another in small Spanish and great expressive gesture. Before we part Lucía asks me for money "to buy some fruit." Xenia approaches Annette and asks for her watch. Later, when we try to process our feelings about the destitution of these women's lives and how hard it is for us to imagine that our presence can mean anything substantial to them, we are troubled by the two women's requests. Neither Annette nor I responded positively to them. We are unsure how we feel about making gifts to some but not all. Beth says it seems reasonable to her that these women asked us for things. She wonders why it surprised us. We take a moment to wonder as well.

We ride a second-class bus from Chichicastenango down to Chimaltenango. These popular forms of transportation are the old Blue Birds of castoff U.S. school bus fame—or notoriety, depending upon your experience. Fixed seats built for two bodies customarily carry three in this nation of people who are generally small in physical size. Bags, parcels, chickens, and an occasional pig are common travelers as well. And in the narrow aisle between the rows another line of riders are wedged in between the overlapping thighs of those to right and left.

The driver is all composure, maneuvering the top-heavy vehicle around hairpin curves past the breathtaking lushness of this country. Low clouds dripping into valleys or the fragmented sight of a volcanic cone rising from a brilliant lake occasionally come into view. Climbing over and pushing his way between bodies in the overflowing aisle, the driver's helper moves back and forth, never forgetting to collect a fare from someone who has boarded or to remind someone else it's time to get off.

In spite of our diversity we women from the United States are generally big. We know that we occupy almost twice the room of our Guatemalan counterparts. Yet people are mostly good natured, courtesy and hospitality being essentials of the Indian culture. The ubiquitous boom box blares from a seat near the back. On this particular ride I have squeezed in beside a young woman—dressed in Ladino clothing—whose three- or four-year-old sleeps by the window while she shifts an infant on her lap. This appears to be a prize seat, only very meagerly occupied, and I smile and wonder if the woman can make an inch or two more room for me?

She informs me flatly that she cannot. Or will not. Her anger is thinly masked, her body rigid. From behind us, a male voice: "Hey, move over for the foreigner. There's room enough." But she cuts him off: "I hate every last one of them," she proclaims to the man who has spoken and anyone close enough to hear. What I have dreamed and dreamed again, always just beneath the surface of my fear, has finally happened; I am being targeted by the endemic resentment born of five hundred years of occupation.

The trip to Chimaltenango will take four and a half hours. I try to reason with my seatmate but she will not address me directly. I am literally sitting on air, and although logic tells me that the bodies around me will most likely prevent my slipping to the baseboards, a sense of imminent unbalance urges me to try, without physically hurting the woman who "hates every last one" of us, to achieve a bit more claim to my territory.

But I cannot.

Each time the bus hugs a curve, its entire contents shifting to the right, my opponent—for that is how she has defined herself—intentionally jabs my ribs. When things slam in the opposite direction I try not to lose ground. Unwillingly my eyes fill with tears. I am reminded of a scene which has inhabited my inner landscape since 1974.

Back then two women from the United States traveled through what was still North Vietnam. Everywhere we were greeted with that special tenderness only the most dignified of nations under attack can offer to visitors from the country trying to wipe them from the map. I was continually amazed at the love we were shown. But one morning we stood beside our jeep as a ferry brought us across a river whose bridge had been bombed out for the twentieth time. A peasant woman asked our translator where the tall women were from. I recognized the response: that word I had come to understand means America. For an instant the woman's eyes held the deepest hatred I had ever seen. Then—the instant controlled —she smiled, all courtesy once more, and turned away.

I have never forgotten the look in that Vietnamese woman's eyes nor my feeling of helplessness and frustration before the inevitable. We had come from the country that was murdering her people; why should she receive our presence with warmth?

Now, on this Guatemalan bus I struggle to find a way out of the same utter frustration. Nothing I say or do makes a difference. The elbow war continues. Then, fifteen or twenty minutes before our destination, a place opens up one row behind me. An elderly man who has witnessed the situation from the beginning literally pulls me back over other bodies to safer space.

Eager to vindicate his country's hospitality, my sudden savior assures me that "most Guatemalans aren't like that." Then his comments take what seems to be a peculiar turn. "If she had been *una india* (an Indian woman)," he insists, "she wouldn't have acted like she did. Only Ladinos are so crude." The Indian, prime target of racist hate, is proudly telling me his people do not behave in such a way. Pondering this I descend from the bus with more on my mind than even the confrontation with my seat mate has provoked.

We are crowded into a small smoky meeting room whose walls are papered with political posters, familiar images of resistance and struggle. But familiar from where? And to whom? After our group's more discreet gatherings in convents and community centers, this decor surprises—and so does the atmosphere. The place is home to the offices of a labor union, male-dominated activity with its characteristic noise and agitation levels. People smoke, and the air is thick. Our meeting is frequently interrupted by men who need one or another of the women gathered with us to answer a question, make a call, type a letter.

The women seem accustomed to such interruptions. Rosita, Olga, Chíquis, Carmen, Sonia, and Blanca belong to what they call the Women's Coordinating Council. They represent the women's caucus of UITA (Geneva-based International Union of Food and Allied Workers, IUF), GRUPEPROMEFAM (Women's Group for Family Improvement), TIERRA VIVA (Living Earth, a feminist organization), and the María Chinchilla Women's Institute. As in our other meetings, we introduce ourselves around the circle and agree upon how we will share experiences in both directions.

We know that Guatemala's women's movement as such is the least developed in Central America. The contradictions—some provoked, others real—between the Indian and Ladina women are a factor. Four decades of brutal repression, affecting women and children in special ways, also cannot be disregarded. Yet as our visit to this country unfolds, we U.S. women speak among ourselves about our persistent sense that something extraordinary is happening among women here. Church women, community organizers, health workers, teachers, women who work in private homes, female members of grass-roots mixed organizations, as well as those who come together exclusively as women: all exude an energy that seems to signal a rejection of previous and unsuccessful male models, a shared attempt at a new type of organization.

Feminism. What does this term mean in a culture where a non-Western tradition fuels many Indian women's lives? Guatemalan women won the vote in 1945. Suffrage, however, has rarely meant much in the political life of this country. Strong female organization took root with the Guatemalan Women's Alliance, a group of teachers and working women who came together during the brief decade of democracy, 1944-54. Later groups were mostly limited to upper-class and professional women until the Christian Democratic government of Vinicio Cerezo opened a measure of political space and peasant and working women began to organize in greater numbers. GAM (Mutual Support Group, led by women and made up of the family members of the disappeared) and CONAVIGUIA (National Coordinating Council of Guatemalan Widows) are human rights organizations that have placed women squarely at the center of the country's resistance struggle.

Our meeting heats up as women open to one another. Our community health workers compare notes with theirs. As always the subjects of alcoholism, rape, battery, and child sexual abuse are common threads. Homelessness, freedom of choice, incest and Satanic Ritual abuse, drugs and the top-heavy war against them, are realities that occupy us north of the border. In Guatemala, rampant illiteracy, high infant mortality, desperate poverty, and rapidly increasing violence are problems for which there are no official answers. Not even close. Death, disappearance, displacement, refugee—these have become ordinary household words.

Then one of the *Tierra Viva* women looks at me. "Margaret," she says, "I want to tell you that nine years ago an Argentinean friend gave me one of your books. I couldn't have said I was a feminist then. But history and experience have taught us. Today I proudly call myself a feminist." For several moments we hold one another with our eyes. For me, the women who have spoken on the pages of my books are talking to each other again.

It is almost the end of our time here. We are waiting for the waiter to bring us dinner at Antojitos, a *comida típica* (native food) place near our hotel. This is a Central American chain; I remember how I loved eating at Managua's Antojitos when I lived in Nicaragua. But we're not talking Burger King or Kentucky Fried Chicken. For me Guatemalan food is always a delight. The fried black beans are my favorite: a succulent loaf from which portions are sliced and served with cream. As in most of Latin America, corn is basic. The *tortillas* are small in size and slightly thicker than their Mexican counterparts.

We are at the tired end of one more very intense day, and as has begun to happen between us we find ourselves asking some version of the question that is always just beneath the surface. What to do? What can we do about these lives, this place, this misery and violence so much a part of the status quo that our own government policy promotes around the world?

At home most of us are involved in solidarity work and those who aren't know they will be now. A number of the women with whom we've spoken have told us about their projects: women's weaving cooperatives, a health clinic in a shanty town where nothing will change until a sewage system is installed (and only the Guatemalan government can do that), the sisters' goats in San Andrés, a widows' sewing project in Cobán. Here in Guatemala City the women of *Tierra Viva* have asked us to read their literature, offer criticisms of their work.

Yes, we will keep in touch with these women and their efforts. We know the contact will nourish us far more than it can them. But our real job as women from the United States is to work on exposing and changing our government's relationship with the government of Guatemala.

Since 1983 the United States has backed Guatemala's attempt to improve its international image and secure multilateral funding. We have injected the country with a large dose of economic assistance in the form of balance-of-payments consideration. In what are called the conflict areas we have given development assistance and local currency funding in support of the military-controlled pacification campaign (otherwise known as *La violencia*, The Violence). Our support of export crops (like the sesame seeds for Big Mac buns) has undermined the people's traditional planting and made their hunger worse. And our military aid, which has increased in spite of occasional complaints from Congress, heavily underwrites the Guatemalan government's counterinsurgency efforts, making the country ever more dependent upon the United States.

It is this information we must help to disseminate at home, against an Establishment media that is thoroughly aligned with such government policy. The enormity of the task assaults my mind and my eyes wander about this dining room. At the other tables: occasional tourists like ourselves, but mostly Guatemalans, families or groups of friends. A woman in *traje* and with stoic face makes corn *tortillas* over an open fire. I think of all the vast differences in our relationships to what is happening here, the living of it, the assignment of responsibility. And I long for a different language, brand new words with which to say what must be said.

—September, 1990

Notes

1. Earlier and partial versions of this piece appeared in The American Voice #24, Fall 1991 ("Color Is Part of What This Black and White Picture is About" pp.42-47) and in On The Issues, Vol. XXI Winter 1991 ("Invasion and Resistance, Guatemalan Women Speak" pp. 16-19 cont.38-39).

2. In 1984, upon my return from 23 years in Latin America, the U.S. Immigration and Naturalization Service (INS) ordered me deported because of the critical nature of some of my writings. Under the 1952 McCarran-Walter Act, it accused me of being "against the good order and happiness of the United States." I chose to fight rather than leave. What followed was a battle that lasted almost five years, and in which I was joined by many prominent writers, artists, feminists, academics, religious orders, unions, and others. We won the case in August of 1989, setting a public opinion (if not a legal) precedent for similar outcomes in other cases—and preparing the stage for a major change in U.S. immigration law.

3. The right wing's habit of disappearing revolutionaries and sometimes even ordinary citizens is endemic to the last three decades of Latin American struggle. People are taken off the streets or pulled from their homes in the middle of the night: bayonets drawn, jeep engines running and lights blaring. Then they are not seen again. The lack of a body keeps loved ones searching, semi-hopeful. Psychologically, a person who is disappeared is more likely to provoke emotional breakdown in a community than a person whose body can be buried and mourned.

4. *I, Rigoberta Menchú: An Indian Woman in Guatemala*, Edited and introduced by Elisabeth Burgos-Debray (London: Verso, 1984). Publication of this book and also my own visit to Guatemala preceded Rigoberta Menchú being awarded the 1992 Nobel Peace Prize.

5. Since this writing, both women were forced to flee Guatemala. The work at CENTROCAP, however, managed to survive.

Additional Sources

The Central America Fact Book by Tom Barry and Deb Preusch, New York, Grove Press, 1986.

Guatemala, A Country Guide by Tom Barry, Albuquerque, The Inter-Hemispheric Research Center, 1989.

I, Rigoberta Menchu, edited and introduced by Elisabeth Burgos-Debray, London, Verso, 1986.

Granddaughters of Corn by Marilyn Anderson and Jonathan Garlock, Willimantic, Connecticut, Curbstone Press, 1988.

2

The Creation of
A Regional Woman
Debbie Ewens of Belize

＊

Debbie Ewens is dark-skinned and stately, her presence nurtured by a racial mix not immediately decipherable to my ignorant North American eye. At the Latin American Studies Association where she attends a panel I am on, I spot her in the audience: tall, with great dignity, the intensity in her eyes speaking louder than her rather conservative dress. When it is time for questions she raises her hand. But hers isn't a question as much as a plea; "Why is Belize never included—rarely even mentioned—when we speak of women in Central America? Please, you must see that we exist!"

Later we talk briefly. I tell her I'd love to hear her story, and the story of women in her country. We exchange addresses, telephone numbers, faxes. A few days later I send a series of questions. My hope is that this may be a beginning, to be built upon by communication over the following months. All I get is silence, a deepening of the distance between our worlds. Well, I rationalize, it was only a chance encounter.

Then, two weeks before I must send my typescript to the publisher, just after midnight in the dry heat of an Albuquerque summer, my fax begins issuing pages of tiny print. Here is Debbie's story, written as if spoken, in passionate prose.

Immediately I try to call. For hours all I get is the repetition of that recorded message we've all heard so often: "We are sorry. Your call did not go through. Please hang up and try again." I have to know if Debbie is willing and able to work with

65

me, in the minimal time we have left. An AT & T operator finally puts me through, seemingly without problem. Debbie Ewens
agrees to drop everything for the next few days and immerse
herself in the telling of her story.

Belize is tucked up into the extreme northeast corner of
Central America. It is divided from Mexico by the Río Hondo
and shares a long western border with Guatemala, from which
over the years it has suffered frequent claims to territorial rights.
Known until 1973 as British Honduras, its 8,866 square miles
(about the size of New Hampshire) remained a colony until its
fairly recent independence in 1981. Its less than 200,000 inhabitants make it the least populated country on the isthmus.

Like a number of other very small nations, Belize has managed to preserve a relatively peaceful internal situation. There
are none of the painful disputes or brutal struggles so common
among the other Central American countries, none of the guerrilla wars, urban or rural. There is little crime, little visible
poverty. Yet the country lacks the capacity to diagnose cancer or
to treat it with chemotherapy or radiation, among much else in
the way of twentieth-century technology. Tom Barry, in his useful book about Belize, characterizes it as follows: "In a recent
newspaper article entitled 'Pesky Bicycles' the writer asserted
that 'Grown men and boys can be seen disregarding traffic laws
on their bikes.' Although Belize is growing, traffic—either
motor or bike—has not yet become an urgent concern. The
small country, after all, does not yet have one traffic light."[1]

Belize is a nation of contrasts. Its mountainous region
along the Guatemalan border boasts unspoiled forests which are
home to exotic animals: jaguars, tapirs, crocodiles, and many
species of birds. Its people descend from Mayan Indians,
Garífuna (or Black Caribs), African slaves, Spanish-speaking
mestizo immigrants from Mexico and other parts of Central
America, East Indians, Middle-Eastern immigrants, and a small
number of caucasians from further north or east.

By the late seventeenth century, pirates, English loggers
(called Baymen), Spaniards, and kidnapped Africans had joined

the native indigenous groups to begin to form what is today a powerful racial and cultural mix. The English established colonial control, eventually permitting a semi-autonomous political model. The People's Unity Party (PUP) is primarily social democratic, although anticommunist and ambivalent about, if not resentful of, U.S. influence in the region.

After independence, the PUP made George Price the country's first prime minister. He has advocated for "wise capitalism." Later the growth of the United Democratic Party (UDP) provided competition, rounding out a conventional two-party system. There have been smaller configurations, left as well as right, but none of any weight.

So Belize remains a stalwart of internal peace, with a foreign policy largely dictated by its ties to Britain and the United States. It flaunts a degree of formal independence through membership in the movement of Non-aligned Nations and a long-time recognition of such groups as the Palestine Liberation Organization. It has remained rather removed from Central American politics, preferring to think of itself as the "Caribbean beat in the heart of Central America" (the slogan of its only radio station).

Internally, although extreme poverty and people's movements for social change are not obvious, there is a high unemployment rate (18% according to Barry), and only 11% of the workforce is organized. Different sources give a picture of a rather staid though laid-back society, doing its best to keep under wraps the sorts of social problems that present a poor public image or may motivate real political challenge. Family is important. Religion is important and actively involved in community control.

Debbie Ewen's story seems both commonplace and unique. Commonplace because it traces the life of a woman schooled and nurtured in all the usual ways. Unique because, as is true of so many women in so many different places, the creativity and independent thought of centuries shines through. Here then is the life of a mixed-blood woman of Belize. Or, as she says, a woman who is Belizean-Nicaraguan, Nicaraguan-Belizean. And through hers there emerges the more general story of women in that ignored Central American nation.

Our method was for me to ask some initial questions, she to respond, me to come back with others, and she to move out along rich pathways of memory until we emerged with a weave about which we both felt comfortable. This is a story about borders, about conquest, assimilation, resistance, and survival:

"My parents created a regional woman."

I was born in one Central American country and reared to be the offspring of another. I identify with both, feel both their rhythms deep beneath my skin. I am Belizean-Nicaraguan. I am Nicaraguan-Belizean. I am not two people in one nor do I suffer an identity crisis. I guess I am simply an early prototype of what was to eventually happen throughout Central America.

Without realizing what they were doing, Charles and Grace Ewens, my parents, created a regional woman. My nationality was partially submerged. It surfaces only on official documents. But I am of an astounding cultural mix. My father is the son of a Maya/Black woman and of a Scottish/Black man. He was born on the Mexican border and reared in Belize, then known as British Honduras. He left Belize at the age of 15 to join the merchant marines; and moved from the Americas to the Far East, to the Orient, and all ports in between. On one of his trips to Bluefields, Nicaragua he met first my Miskita/Black grandmother, who took pity on the young man spitting blood on the sidewalk after an obvious visit to the nearby dentist. She took him home, doctored him, and introduced him to the daughter she'd had with my Black/Miskita/Chinese grandfather.

The black-haired, slant-eyed young woman was not a stranger to my father. He had first seen her in a photograph that belonged to one of his fellow crew members—a cousin of my mother's. When he set eyes on that photograph, my father told my mother's cousin that the day would come when he would meet and marry the woman in the picture. I have been told that he would often borrow that photograph and disappear into his cabin. I suspect that my father was already in love with my mother when they met. Only hours later he asked her to marry him. The following day his formal request arrived by letter. And two years later he did marry the very protected, very loved young woman he had first seen in a photograph.

"My mother would never consider herself to be progressive. I do."

By the time my parents turned 27 I was a part of their life. And I believe my father's decision to leave the sea and settle down to fatherhood and Belize had to do with my arrival. He became a Customs Boatman, earning $95.00 ($47.50 U.S.) a month. The salary was a very very far cry from what he had earned at sea.

The Customs Department was also my introduction to a man's world. My mother would never consider herself to be progressive. I do. She made me a miniature copy of my father's uniform, cut from one of his older uniform shirts. It was an emotional gesture but, unofficially, made me the youngest and the only female boat person I have ever heard of in the department. Unfortunately, I have few real memories of that time. But as I grew up I realized that I was very comfortable in the company of men, that I was not afraid to voice my opinions, that I held opinions about everything, and that many of them were not mainstream.

My mechanical engineer father utilized every single thing he could find and taught me how to create something from nothing, while my mother was engaged in a constant campaign to open me to the academic world. I was growing in ways and doing things that other women of my generation weren't. My very traditional parents were creating an independent thinker, a maverick if you like. I don't believe they were aware of that.

At the same time I was being taught the genealogy, the customs, the silent nuances, the subtle shades and gradations of my other country. In time my parents gave me a sister and then a brother. The unstructured lessons became much more defined. I was taught the who, what, when, where, and why of the Nicaraguan lifestyle. I was made to understand the importance of my older-child status. In an emergency it was my obligation and mine alone to see that we all got home. I spoke Spanish. I sang the national and traditional Nicaraguan songs.

I speak of myself as being of Miskito (Miskitu) heritage, because it is easier for you to understand. The truth is, I share the heritage of the Waiknas. My ancestors lived along the coast of Nicaragua, known to you as the Mosquito Coast. Long ago someone probably adapted the name of the Moschitu River—located near Cabo Gracias a Dios—to an entire coastline and people. Hence the Mosquito Coast and the people of Mosquitia, or Miskitos.

"You need to understand the stigma and discrimination that afflicted my people."

I do not know many Nicaraguan-Belizean women with Miskito bloodlines. When I read Belizean history I realize that there was quite a bit of contact between Belize and Bluefields, Nicaragua. Many Miskito men worked in the logging camps of British Honduras and many of them settled here. Those men became totally assimilated. It doesn't seem odd to me that those Miskito loggers slid into the Belizean culture; it had everything to do with survival.

You need to understand the stigma and discrimination that afflicted my people. Those loggers were not known as Miskitos; they were called Whitkas. A corruption of Waikna? In Belize Whitka is a derogatory label. The impression I've gotten over the years is that way back then we were considered a low-down lot. This has survived. The social perception of the Miskitos was so shabby that when my mother first came to Belize she was advised it would be best to keep her heritage hidden. She refused to do so.

Years later my mother's Miskito origins brought my parents face to face with a diabolical comment. My aunt, upon meeting my very beautiful, very Miskito-looking toddler sister for the first time, questioned my father—her brother—in company of friends: "Where did this little coolie (East Indian) one come from? We have no coolies in our family," she said.

Time has not changed the Belizean prejudice against the Miskitos. My brother, sister, and I had a tutor who I can say without reservation admired and respected us. But the day came when even he questioned our "coolie" appearance. We explained that we are of Miskito origin. I will never forget the questions that followed. He was convinced that Miskitos were Garífunas (Black Caribs, a group discriminated against for years) and that we possessed strange abilities linked to the occult and cannibalism. Was I too young to recognize discrimination? Or had I been taught that there was just too much of everything mixed up inside me to split racial hairs? Very patiently, as best I could, I tried to explain who and what we were. Today my reaction would be quite different.

To get back to those Miskito loggers, they settled with their Belizean women and began their families along the highways of the country, and in small, sparsely populated riverside villages. Their children and grandchildren know nothing of the Miskito way of life and I am convinced that many are not even aware of their cultural mix. Perhaps I am a minority. Perhaps not. If I appear to be a rarity I think it is simply because I have willingly accepted who and what I am. My mother never felt she needed to deny her heritage.

Five years ago my sister married an extended cousin of ours whose cultural mix is Miskito/Black/German. Together they have two very beautiful Nicaraguan-Belizean daughters with clearly defined physical traits of their Miskito heritage. We are beginning to rear another generation that must be educated as we were. I want my nieces to be totally confident. It's just about the only thing that we can give them.

"I was a child when I first saw a photograph of Sandino."

I never believed that there would come a time when no members of my immediate family would be left in Nicaragua. The Sandinista revolution took care of that. I never even considered that there might come a time when as a family we would have no roof under which to sit. Hurricane Joanna bears that responsibility. Now there is only my grandfather living in Pearl Lagoon and a few cousins scattered here and there. Those who have not died have moved to Miami and New York.

I was a child when I first saw a photograph of Augusto César Sandino. It was in an old wooden trunk owned by my great-grandmother. She had pictures of Queen Victoria too, the Royal Family, a Miskito Indian Chief, and an assortment of things which I would probably now consider valuable. My great-grandmother lived at a time when there was no municipal office in Bluefields. As a midwife she was in the habit of noting down in a big black book every birth she attended and their accompanying dates. Years later people would come to her to verify their date of birth when applying for birth certificates or passports.

But I've rambled away from Sandino. It was decades later before I saw another photograph of the man. This time it was on television. We were visiting relatives in Santa Ana, California. The group that the world would eventually refer to as the Sandinistas had just stormed the *Palacio Nacional* in Managua.[2] I saw the image of Sandino and immediately recognized him from the one I had seen in my grandmother's trunk. My father turned to me and said: "You have a memory the size of an elephant's."

In 1979 the owner of that trunk, the great old matriarch of our family, died. She had lived for 106 years. Even now I can see her in her rocking chair, sitting regally erect, smoking one of her god-awful pipes. I hated the smell of those pipes. Mama, as we always called her, would always set aside a few *córdobas* with which to buy the tobacco she stored in a tin can with Henry VIII's face on it. I think it was Henry. Damn, in the light of our history it might well have been Raleigh.

We should have known when we buried her that nothing would be the same again. Times had changed. Bluefields was about to become a different place. A family friend in describing my great-grandmother once said that she was the type of woman who if you told her she was a son-of-a-bitch would reply that you were a god-damned-son-of-a-bitch. She would have clashed violently with Sandinismo. But Augusto César Sandino's arm stretched out from the grave, passed through my great-grandmother's trunk, and touched the nerve center of our family. Suddenly our *barrio*[3] was not as peaceful or as calm as it was before.

I speak of the storm that entered our family home, but it is a storm whose winds did not whip my back, whose uprooted branches did not physically bind me. When I speak like this I am using the speech of my great-grandmother, my aunt, uncles, and cousins. The very purest Nicaraguan essence runs in my veins, and so the revolution took on emotional characteristics in my Belize City neighborhood. It brought feelings of guilt each time I ate, covered myself with a blanket, took a walk in the sunshine. Its second passage penetrated the very walls of my home, pushing them outward and straining every kind of resource as we made way to accommodate our family members who were fleeing for their safety.

"Somehow we understood that neither the Somocistas nor the Sandinistas were interested in who we were."

The general belief is that the people of Nicaragua's Atlantic Coast supported the Contras. In our home the people were just people. They were not supporters of anything or anyone. They only wanted to be left alone. I think somehow we understood that neither the Somocistas nor the Sandinistas were interested in who we were. We were too little, too insignificant. During those years of revolution my grandmother grew tired from her fight with cancer and followed her mother to the grave. At first the war upset me. Then, when my grandmother died, I began hating the people and their cause: that impenetrable barrier between us in Belize and my grandmother in Bluefields.

I heard of my grandmother's death at the Miami International Airport on my way to a conference being hosted in Jamaica that addressed the "problem" of Central American refugees. Later that night in my hotel room I wrote: "Mourning ribbons tie the abdomen of my motherland / weary anguished tears flow freely from her eyes / red blood milk of her swollen breasts / oozing for her sons now dead."

That was the beginning of a tribute to my grandmother.

Now I understand it also as a part of my own struggle. I hated myself for identifying with a country and a heritage that is undoubtedly mine. I was so far away from the gunfire. I did not stand in line day after day to buy food. I could not bury my dead according to our traditions. I had begun to feel an almost certainly permanent separation from people, the things that I loved and that I never doubted loved me in return.

"The girls' father was killed, and we knew nothing would ever be the same."

Even now there are times when I take out that script and read my words. Some of them are so angry. I wrote at a convulsive time in the history of my people. Some of them are full of shame, horror, frustration, and dismay. I wanted to know what it was that had crippled us, why bullets were ripping apart people's insides. Then the girls' father was killed, and we knew nothing would ever be the same.

I speak as though you know the girls. They are the granddaughters of my mother's brother; that makes them my cousins. But they were reared as my sisters. In my heart they, along with a small boy my family took in, have become my children. Now that those girls have grown, they are full of questions. They want to know who their father was. They question the reasons for his death.

They cannot understand that he could simply have attended a party, that suddenly the venue was turned into a sieve by hundreds upon hundreds of bullets, that people had to throw themselves to the ground and that later their father was found with a single bullet hole between his eyes. He was the only casualty of a night of madness.

It wasn't only the death of the girls' father, though, that scarred us, that changed my life. Years ago their grandmother remarried and moved to the Ingenio San Antonio, outside Managua. During the war years, one of her daughters, an auxiliary nurse, was raped. When her mother realized she was pregnant she sent her to Bluefields—to my grandmother, her ex-mother-in-law. They hoped to hide the shame. Today this woman is the mother of a child she finds impossible to love though she wants desperately to do so.

I often think back to that day when an airplane brought to Belize my aunt and two very shy little girls. I find myself thinking that they have had to grow with only a second-hand knowledge of who their parents were. Those girls are among the real casualties of war.

"Have I told you I hate armies?"

The tragedy of the Nicaraguan—not Sandinista—revolution is that the world never understood. How could it? In 1991 the University of Central Arkansas staged my play called "WISOP" (an acronym for Women in Search of Peace). I am told that there were some very angry people with placards outside the campus theater. How could there not have been? The Central American vision of the revolution was so very far removed from North America's comfortable armchair position.

Have I told you that I hate armies? There is something morally wrong with an institution that teaches men to kill while hypocritically upholding codes of honor. Yet I must accept that there was a time when things were simpler. Men who went to war fought visible enemies. Everyone knew who was who, what was what, and what was expected of them. In Central America the war was fought on two fronts: one in plush diplomacy, the other in blood.

I asked uncomfortable questions about Central America. I publicly read my poetry to groups that glorified the revolutionary process, and I challenged anyone willing to present the revolution as a Central American model. My mother is often afraid of the things I write. She cautions me about the fights I pick. She is happiest when my stories are written with children in mind. My political opinions make her uncomfortable and afraid.

"I was not cut out for Government Service."

You ask about my position in Belizean society. Belize has a population of 184,000 persons. Too many of them appear content to take things easy. I hate the idea of taking things easy. But, then, what qualifies me to say that people are content with being laid back? What I classify as laid back could be cultural. It is probably what has saved Belize from the quagmire in which its neighbors have found themselves.

Whether these perceptions are right or wrong, they are part of what made me realize that I was not cut out for Government Service. I cut my journalistic teeth in the newsroom of the country's only radio station. Radio Belize is government owned and controlled. I should have known better. I couldn't function in an atmosphere of control. It took me six months to get out. The decision surprised no one; people were only surprised that I had found a way to stay that long.

After leaving the station I tried freelancing. But the papers too were all politically owned. The choice was to write for the party in office or for the opposition: essentially no choice at all. Since then I have charted an independent professional course. It has allowed me to pioneer in many areas of Belizean journalism. I realized that when I held in my hands the Journalism Award for my television show on the subject of AIDS.

I live at home, with my parents. I must do so until I decide to marry. It was on my family dining table that I established Ewens Publications, a one-woman operation. I research, write, produce, sell advertising, and distribute my own publications. I can say whatever I want.

Writing in an atmosphere of freedom is important to me, but I also needed to consider the practical side of life. I needed to pull my weight in the family. So I did what the mono-crop country of Belize should have done: I diversified. During the crisis years in Central America I had worked with a UN subsidiary, the Intergovernmental Committee for Migration, which resettled Central American refugees to Canada. Later I took what I had learned at ICM and used it to recruit and screen personnel for cruise liners.

"I live in one of Belize City's more economically depressed and violent neighborhoods."

A year later I invested in a small garment manufacturing business. These businesses, which I entered for personal financial reasons, also became important in the public sphere. I live in one of Belize City's more economically depressed and violent neighborhoods. From the porch of my family home things seem safe. But the truth is I am surrounded by people who live with haunting poverty.

Exactly half of this nation's population is between the ages of one and seventeen. But according to a UNICEF report, 46% do not complete primary education and 11% of those between the ages of five and fourteen have never seen the inside of a schoolroom. I live on the periphery of an area where over 50% of the households include five persons and where more than 63% have two or fewer bedrooms. These people are anchored in the rawness of the poverty of developing nations; it is sharper, deeper, more intense. The stench is much more offensive. HIV/AIDS, gang violence, escalating crime, single parenthood, teenage pregnancy, and rising unemployment add to the situation.

Once word got out that I was offering jobs overseas, men began crawling out of places of which I'd never heard. Those who qualified, sold the family furniture and television sets so as to be able to travel. Today, five years later, I continue to recruit personnel. I continue to be amazed by the sheer numbers of men who seek jobs in the bellies of ships.

Women came wanting to sew. Painfully, it is harder to fulfill their dreams. It makes me angry each time I have to send a woman away without work. But people here have been conditioned to believe that anything made in the U.S.A. is of superior quality than locally produced clothing. On the other hand I seem to have found a few markets in which Belizeans are not prepared to allow the United States to compete: school uniforms, maternity wear, and burial shrouds. For approximately eighteen hours out of every twenty-four, I write, interview potential crewmembers, and supervise my sewing staff. It's often an incredibly full day.

"I sometimes feel that admitting to being a feminist in this country is tantamount to committing suicide."

You ask about my schooling. I was educated by nuns in an ultra-conservative atmosphere and reared in a morally strict home. I should have become the wife of a respectable professional, mother to his 6.0 children, and a very socially correct hostess. I am none of those things. I sometimes feel that admitting to being a feminist in this country is tantamount to committing suicide.

While Belize remained stuck in a time warp as to the meaning of feminism, Anita Hill gave testimony about sexual harassment on the job. In Belize no one wants to discuss sexual harassment. No one wants to make waves. On U.S. campuses date rape has been opened up and publicly discussed. Belizean law enforcement officers point to last year's 22 reported cases of rape and admit that almost all were cases of acquaintance rape. But Belize does not discuss the subject.

Across North America, Right to Lifers and abortion activists face off. In Catholic Belize, women with retained particles and life-threatening infections following butcher-shop abortions arrive at the Belize City Hospital and are given emergency D and Cs. No one knows the figures related to this issue. In an era of AIDS, in other countries gay activists march and seek rights along with treatment. In Belize I am the only journalist to speak about the subject on a regular basis. I am currently seeking funds to put together a publication I hope to call "HIV Connection", where HIV and AIDS can be addressed. My first half-written article, entitled "Female, Black, Poor, and HIV-Positive" has yet to be seen by the world.

Hillary Clinton is television-familiar to Belizean women. How many see her as a new and continuous part of the feminist evolution? There are no feminist voices in Belizean media, not even mine. Indeed, local media ignore feminist issues. My more radical feminist works are hidden deep inside my desk. I think my family would be supportive, but they would also be embarrassed by poetry that speaks of women excreting the unfertilized semen of their men from their malnourished insides.

"If there's a feminist movement in Belize, it is a covert operation."

Professional and semi-professional women in Belize would perhaps agree that here it is definitely impossible to have one's cake, eat it, and not absorb the calories. Many more Belizean women are now employed than were twenty years ago. Yet many Belizean men continue to prefer a woman willing to remain at home, have his children, clean house, and above all be obedient.

I recently went to a Muslim wedding at which the bride was poetically advised, by another woman, to be the polished floor on which her husband should walk and the comfortable seat on which he should sit. My initial fury when I realized that the women were expected to sit at the back of the room turned to murderous rage as I listened to those words.

The obscurity and archaic visions of feminism in Belize make it difficult to decide if there was ever a formal woman's movement here. I know that many would disagree. But the structure of this society hasn't even permitted a formalized feminist organization, like those in the United States, or their imitations in other Central American or Caribbean countries. If there is a feminist movement in Belize, it is a covert operation. Young women, allowed to study, left for American universities and then returned home—with degrees and feminist ideas. These ideas scared potential mates and family members. Mothers cautioned about the need to pretend to be stupid and humble if one wanted to find a husband.

No, it definitely was not a formalized movement that brought about whatever change Belizean women now enjoy. It took savvy, intuition, perhaps even clairvoyance to institute and create domestic versions of imported and unpopular feminist ideas. On the other hand, there is the possibility that there was always an undeclared feminist movement alive in this country. Historically, Belizean women have held their families together. Belizean society is the result of a forest economy. Men would leave for months to cut logs or extract chicle. The women remained at home with their children, struggling without funds, baking bread and taking in laundry to make ends meet. And at the end of each season the men returned to drink out the meager earnings, beat their wives, rule the roost, and finally leave the women behind again, pregnant with yet more children.

I think that the first glimpse of some sort of feminist movement here crawled out of the male-dominated political parties. Traditionally, women have long been involved in the political process; they were the underlings. Then somehow the manipulators of the political machinery began to realize the importance of addressing the new, young, academic elite. This necessarily meant presenting a feminist agenda. But the women pushed forward lacked the vibrancy, spice, and boldness to effectively utilize this agenda and springboard a feminist movement. They lacked the leadership to conduct, manage, and direct a movement capable of creating a new social and political equation, one that involved women.

It is possible to argue that many of Belize's NGOs are women's organizations. I question this. They are tied to the government's Department of Women's Affairs. These NGOs have been visibly active around issues such as the Domestic Violence Act, organizations like Belize's Family Life Association, and the National Organization for the Prevention of Child Abuse. But, for example, where were the masses of Belizean women when the Domestic Violence Act was being presented?

I guess I conclude that there is a quasi-feminist movement in Belize. It's not a movement that seeks to embrace the female population. The poor social conditions may be what makes it so passive. It's important to remember that to declare oneself feminist is to risk being labeled lesbian. Those who sign the bills into law are men with egos that must be stroked.

"Social perceptions did not allow for a vision of women who were sexually involved with anyone but men."

You ask me to speak about lesbianism in Belize, but I must admit I cannot do so with much authority. My only contact with homosexuality has come about as a result of my work with HIV and AIDS. Much of what I can say will be from conversations for a biography of a very courageous man who allowed me to push him forward and publicly admit his HIV status.

I'm not sure I knew any homosexual men during my childhood. The only information I had was what I overheard. Adults would suddenly change the subject when they became aware you were listening. That was especially true during my childhood in Nicaragua. I am, however, sure that I never knew or even heard of a lesbian woman. For whatever reason, male homosexuality could be whispered about while lesbians were not even mentioned. Could it be that social perceptions did not allow for a vision of women who were sexually involved with anyone but men?

The arrival of AIDS to Belizean shores stripped the lace curtain from this little bible-carrying society. Andrés—my HIV-positive friend—believes that AIDS is a liberating force for those in the closet here. He feels that although the price is high, it is one that must be paid for future generations. And when he speaks of future generations he's not referring only to gay and lesbian persons but straight people as well. Belize, like the rest of Central America and the Caribbean, frequently forces gay men to marry straight women who must suffer without a word.

Out with Andrés I have observed that male homosexuality is stronger and better organized than a lesbian movement here. I'm sure this society also forces lesbians into heterosexual relationships in protection of themselves, their jobs, and their families. But despite the relative strength of a gay male presence, it has been impossible to form support groups for persons with AIDS. In Belize there's no such thing as a support group for HIV-positives. Andrés tells me: "No body want no body else know sch dem gat AIDS. The goddamn fool dem can't see sch all a we di dead. We gat to hide and be Mr. this and Miss Dat. Till this thing cat out we backside." Even the level of discrimination within the clinics themselves is astounding.

I mentioned attending that Muslim wedding. I was the only unmarried woman there. Interestingly enough, one Muslim woman took it upon herself to warn me that it was of extreme urgency that I be married. She said I risked becoming a lesbian simply because I operate within professional channels. Her comment was an effective reflection of Belizean society. The lesbian label is used against women here who have decided to spend time working on their careers and leaving family life for the future.

—Summer, 1994

Notes

1. *Belize, a Country Guide* by Tom Barry, Albuquerque, The Inter-Hemispheric Education Resource Center, 1990.
2. August, 1978. A commando led among others by Dora María Téllez took some 3,500 people hostage. After successful negotiations with the Somoza regime, they were able to gain a large sum of money, publication of political information, and the release of all political prisoners then in custody.
3. Neighborhood.

3

"The Feminist Movements in Latin America Possess an Originality, a Creativity and a Force that Allow them to Speak with Authority in the Struggle with the North"

Interview with Magaly Pineda

✳

Magaly Pineda is without doubt one of the leading Latin American feminists. She is an expansive and energetic woman who exudes delight: delight in living and in making life more livable for others. There's always laughter with Magaly, and those whispered confidences reminiscent of our teenage years but filled today with the more interesting gossip of women's camaraderie. One of our growing feminist breed for whom theory and practice are inextricably linked, she has been a moving presence in the southern hemisphere and beyond for many of her more than fifty years.

I met Magaly in the early 1980s, at a women's seminar in Mexico City. Since then, we've seen each other in Nicaragua and most recently in Atlanta, Georgia at the yearly meeting of the Latin American Studies Association (LASA). Our encounters are always filled with the immediacy and passion that feminists bring to one another and to what we do: instant recognition, a certain intimacy, compassion, humor. I knew in Atlanta that an interview with this woman was long overdue. Getting her to talk about her life would also be a way of looking at feminism in the Dominican Republic.

In the months that followed—the LASA meeting was in April, 1994—we communicated by phone, letter, and fax. I sent questions; Magaly responded with thoughtful answers, attempting to offer the flavor as well as the meaning of her movement. Her commitment to this project was such that it seems most productive simply to offer the fullness of her voice. What follows, then, is an almost verbatim[1] rendering:

"The doctor told my father I was a girl; he said, 'Impossible!'"

Jesus, Margaret, I never thought it would take me so long to get around to sitting down with you to share this "cup of coffee"! These are frantic times. I think I mentioned that we're embroiled in an electoral campaign here, the elections are May 16th. My husband is running for Congress on the ticket of the main opposition Party.[2] And here at CIPAF[3] we're up to our necks with work on an important project aimed at promoting women's political participation. Our main goal is that our demands, our gender demands, be included in the different party platforms. It seems like I never stop running.

And another thing: searching for time to savor this metaphorical cup of coffee I've become aware of how hard it is—in our culture—to take any time for oneself, even a few moments alone are hard to come by. Sometimes I think I only get to be alone when I sleep. Because my house is always filled with people…and then I'm at the office most of the day…or I'm out with friends. We just don't have our own time. And I guess I'm used to this pace. I don't even long to be alone until I try to find a few moments for something like this interview, time to sit down with your questions.

You ask me to talk about my origins, the family I was born into, where and when. Well, I was born in 1943, March 21st. I've been told that my father wanted to name me Spring but fortunately had a last minute change of heart and I became Magaly. Magaly was the heroine of a novel my mother was reading while she was pregnant with me. Antonia—my middle name and one I almost never use—is for my grandmother, who was called Antonieta. I might have preferred Antonieta.

When he was quite young my father moved to the capital, to Santo Domingo where I was born. He actually came to study for the priesthood, but changed his mind; which was fortunate because my father, to the end of his days, remained a lover of women, of all the carnal pleasures. But his seminary time did give him a solid education, probably the best he could have gotten at the time. My father was born in 1903. It was hard to get a decent education back then.

My mother was born in 1916. She was an only child, her father was a land-owner in the central part of the country. Later he lost his money, and went on to have many other children by his second wife. My maternal grandmother's only child was my mother. That grandmother married late, and she gave birth to my mother when she was already considered *jamona*, a derogatory term used here when speaking about women who married beyond their teens.[4] So my mother received abundant love from her mother. My grandmother was a mulatto woman, daughter of a mulatto mother whose grandfather was jet black. So black in fact, that she tells me that as a child when she saw him in the street she would hide—so as not to have to say he was her grandfather. I mention this because the subject of Caribbean racism will surely come up throughout this conversation.

My mother only went through fifth grade, which in her time was actually considered a lot for a woman. When she and my father married they wanted children, and for many years waited for them to come. My father had already had three, with women he didn't marry. You know what a common thing that is in our society. For years my mother underwent one treatment after another; she went to doctors but she also explored the more traditional routes. She went to midwives and to witches:

anything to be able to get pregnant.

Finally, after all those years of trying, she gave birth to her first, a son. How they loved that boy! And then all of a sudden, in a matter of days, he died of meningitis. He was ten months old. My parents always said that their pain was so great they can't remember the funeral. Friends, neighbors, godparents were the ones who dealt with the wake and all the other arrangements.

My mother then became a woman who was perennially sad. She dressed in black. She would get up early each day and go down to the cemetery where she'd spend hours and hours. My father would pick her up for lunch, but she'd go back in the afternoon. And she wouldn't leave that graveside until the cemetery gates closed.

In her grief my mother wanted nothing to do with the world of the living. And of course sex was the furthest thing from her mind. Every time my father came near her she tried to reject his advances. But in the midst of that attempted rejection she realized one day she was pregnant again. My mother considered the pregnancy an affront to the memory of her dead son, and she tried to get an abortion.

That unwanted child was me.

My arrival into this world, then, not only meant my mother's victory over a long depression; it also marked the beginning of my father's depression. Because up to then he'd only had boys. His first three children were male, and then the child he and my mother lost. My father was extremely macho, a womanizer of the worst sort, and he was very clear about the fact that he didn't want daughters. My mother always excused him by saying it was because he knew what happened to girls.

So when I was born and the doctor told my father he had a daughter, he said "Impossible!" He tried to find out if maybe another child had been born at the same time and they'd been switched, anything not to have to accept the fact that his newborn was a girl. My mother says my father spent the whole first month of my life going to my crib, opening my diaper, looking at my genitalia and exclaiming: "Impossible!"

"I too wanted to be a nun."

Still, in time my parents managed to overcome their shared grief. My father managed to overcome his expectations, and—on that block in a city that at the time couldn't have had more than half a million inhabitants—I became everybody's toy. I have dozens of photographs that tell the story of my infancy, an extremely happy time surrounded by the love of my parents and of an almost infinite number of godparents and friends. Because in those days the custom wasn't just your birth godparents, but your baptismal godparents, your confirmation godparents.... And of course your godfathers and godmothers were an integral part of your family.

I remember Christmas, or Three Kings Day. We didn't just await the gifts those kings left beneath our beds; we'd also go to visit our godparents, aunts, uncles, cousins, to receive the presents left for us there.

At the time of my birth, my father worked in a pharmacy. Shortly thereafter he started representing pharmaceutical imports at the same firm. He traveled a lot. I remember his returns from each of those trips as moments of great joy. My father had a magical way about him, he could make the most ordinary event into something special, something marvelous. From those trips he'd always bring some surprise: a firefly in a jar, and he'd turn out the lights and we'd watch as it came to life. Or a clock on which a long-footed bird would come out and chirp the hour.... My father had a great imagination, a great sense of play.

After my father's first shock at having had a girl, there were two subsequent shocks. My sisters Milagros and Maritza were born in quick succession. Milagros and I are only 11 months apart. For many years we were a trio, they dressed us alike, and if it hadn't been for that racial mix so characteristic of the Caribbean, we might have seemed like triplets. I was plump, with straight hair and brown eyes. Milagros was tall and thin, with huge green eyes, but her hair was tightly curled, leaving no doubt as to her African heritage. The youngest, Maritza, is a

87

light-skinned mulatto with jet black hair and very caucasian features. So, even though our closeness in age made us seem like triplets, our physical features and our temperaments were very different.

Throughout our childhoods we three shared a bedroom. We were always dressed alike. We were given the same toys. And we shared our father with his magical imagination, and a mother who was very spirited, excelled at commerce, and had a great deal of personal initiative.

As a young girl I studied with Franciscan nuns. It was one of the two most exclusive schools in Santo Domingo.[5] Although we might say my parents were lower middle class at that time, they both held onto memories of aristocratic backgrounds. My father's was one of the important families in the southern part of the country. And my mother always talked about her grandparents and great-grandparents who had taken part in the struggles for independence in the 1860s. So, although they didn't have all that much money at the time, our parents struggled to give us good educations and to try to connect us with the higher echelons of society.

I was educated with nuns from the age of five. I have pleasant memories of those years. It was a girls' school, of course, and the nuns, well some of them were warm and kind, others were difficult. But I found a core encouragement to learn, a great emphasis on knowledge. Certain of the nuns were extremely dedicated to teaching. They wanted more for us than what was normally expected of a girl in those years.

During my early schooling, and particularly after I took my first communion, I became a mystic. I too wanted to be a nun. Oh yes, I wanted to be a martyr. I wanted to go on a mission to Alaska, to save little Black children in Africa, I dreamed about all those mission stories the nuns told us.

I can still remember a sermon I heard when I was nine; a priest who visited the school spoke to us about the terrors of hell. And since I was aware of the fact that my father wasn't a practicing Catholic and I knew he could be relegated to that hell, my mysticism reached levels that threatened my health.

In complicity with one of the nuns I began to make small sacrifices, like putting pebbles in my shoes so that God would show my father the light and he would mend his ways. That nun let me kneel on a stone floor behind one of those big old wardrobes, also as a sacrificial act. And she helped, with her prayers and rosaries. It was the two of us in a secret pact, attempting to save my father's soul. I was nine, but she wasn't that much older; she was just seventeen. For years that nun was the center of my existence.

Sister Dorotea—that was her name—was suddenly sent to another school one day. And I cried for weeks. The superior must have feared that we were getting too close. Even though we're talking about a nine-year-old child and a childlike woman of seventeen.

Those memories of my girlhood: the marvelous visits to the zoo that seemed like safaris—we'd pretend we were in Africa riding wild horses or picnicking on the Sahara—or the times my father took a beer and a sandwich and served them up in a champagne glass and with great fanfare so they became something utterly "other." My memories of my mother were less romantic, more rigorous during those years. She was the disciplinarian, the one who made us do our homework, the one who pressured us constantly to do better, to be all we could be. She was the bad guy in the film.

"'Well,' he said, 'we're going to read.'"

And as we grew, the relationship with my father also became stronger, intellectually. Because when I was seven years old I had another experience which was to have a big influence on my life. That wasn't just the year of my first communion; we also moved. We moved—on my mother's initiative—to one of the principal commercial streets in the city, where mother proudly opened her first store. That store was named after me and it sold a little of everything: children's clothes, notions, ribbons.... It was located in a very good spot and quickly became a prosperous business.

Right across the street from mother's store was the largest and most important bookstore in the country. And I quickly made friends with its owner. His name was Don Juan de la Rosa. He was a tall Black man with a resounding voice. He was very intelligent, with a great sensitivity. He'd see me looking at the shelves of books and one day he asked me: "Are you the new neighbor?" I told him I was. "Do you like to read?" I told him I did. "Well," he said, "we're going to read."

First he loaned me children's books, and he always asked me to tell him the stories. Little by little he let me choose the books I wanted. So from the age of seven to around sixteen I had access to the greatest library…without it ever costing me a cent. Needless to say, I read a lot that I didn't understand, like Zola when I was twelve. I had to go to the dictionary to look up the words I didn't know, and so the dictionary too became my friend. And I even read a few books that caught my attention, behind Don Juan de la Rosa's back.

So I grew up among books, nuns, weekly mass, society parties, Sunday strolls along the boardwalk of our beautiful city, outings for ice cream and to the first place that sold hamburgers in Santo Domingo, afternoon matinees. But as I discovered the world of books, that idyllic world my parents gave me began to seem less perfect. One day, when I was twelve, I asked my father: "Why don't we have elections here, like they do in other countries? Why do we always have the same president?"

"The Trujillo dictatorship began in 1931."

The Trujillo dictatorship began in 1931. In a very short time the Trujillo family had taken control of the country, dividing it up among themselves. By the time I was born, Trujillo had such total control over the people that he'd managed to change the name of Santo Domingo—first city of the Americas—to *Ciudad Trujillo*, Trujillo City. That man, who by the '50s was beginning to feel the first cracks in his dictatorship, was exerting an ever greater pressure over Dominican society. Everyone, in one way or another, was beholden to him. Everything was his.

My mother, who frequently traveled to Puerto Rico to buy things for her store, had to apply for her passport. That is, you couldn't keep your passport at home. Each time a person wanted to travel he or she had to apply for a passport, and upon their return had to relinquish it. The city was filled with men—everyone knew who they were, although they weren't in uniform—and those men were virtual spies; they listened, they saw, they checked up on people: anyone who dared show any level of dissent. When I was twelve and I asked my father that question—well, he later told me he'd wondered if he would have the courage to respond honestly. He knew he was risking his life. But he took a chance on me. He said that it was true, we didn't live in a democracy—a word I'd learned from its Greek root—but in a dictatorship. He said Trujillo remained in power because of strict controls, based on fear.

And then my father explained something I'd never really understood completely. Lots of times I remembered he'd said he was going off somewhere, on a trip, but then he'd end up not going. He hadn't been issued a passport. He told me he didn't support Trujillo, that he thought our country deserved something better, but that he didn't feel like he could participate in the struggle against the dictatorship. He couldn't fight against him, but he wouldn't go to the public meetings in support of the man. For 31 years my father waged this sort of passive resistance against the dictatorship. That conversation with my father when I was twelve marked the end of my childhood and the beginning not just of my adolescence but of my maturity.

While my girlfriends at school were beginning to be interested in boys, to go to parties and wear their first bras or womanly underwear, I was reading avidly about other places and other times—and dreaming of something called freedom. My first adolescent poems, which I no longer have, weren't poems about love; they were poems of struggle and in praise of liberty.

Later my political interests were reflected as well among a group of cousins and an uncle of mine; almost by accident we discovered we shared similar ideas. In contrast with our parents, we weren't satisfied with passive resistance. We set small goals for ourselves, incipient ways in which we felt we could help to rouse the population.

Some of our activities were sort of silly, like writing the initials C.T. on the walls of the city—for *Ciudad Trujillo*—which, when written on a wall like that people could read as being against Trujillo. Or we'd reproduce verses of our beautiful national anthem and put them under people's doors, or on the windshields of cars, or—as I once did—place them on the nuns' desks; they'd turn pale with fright when they found them there. With my cousins and particularly with my uncle Manuel those little acts of rebellion grew. We were super critical of the dictatorship.

Someone else who had a big impact on my childhood was my uncle Manuel. He was a heart specialist, a very tall man with a beautiful singing voice who loved Mexican *rancheras* because he had done his medical specialty in Mexico. After all these years I still remember those songs of his. My uncle was like a magnet in our family. He was actually my mother's first cousin. But they were raised together so I didn't find out until many years later that they were cousins, not brother and sister. Uncle Manuel was the center of the Tejada clan—Tejada was my mother's maiden name. He was always getting the family together, a family that he adored. And since he'd been in Mexico during the '40s and '50s, he brought back a love for the Mexican revolution, for the Mexican model: agrarian reform, a system where those who worked the land could own it.

When I was fifteen or so I had a discussion with my father. My uncle Manuel had loudly defended agrarian reform while my father, much to my surprise, argued in defense of private property. I think that was the first time in my life, in that discussion in which the men allowed me to participate, that I openly disagreed with my father. I said I too believed the land should belong to those who worked it. Later, in 1960, my uncle, Dr. Manuel Tejada, would be tortured to death in prison—by Trujillo's henchmen.

The political situation in the Dominican Republic became more and more difficult. By 1955 the profound economic crisis shaped everything. My mother made more frequent trips to Puerto Rico in her attempt to bolster our family income. And it was around that same time that my father not only lost his job but was arrested by the secret police. Thanks to the influence of a godmother and to my aunt—who had connections to a general who had a very bad reputation but was close to the family— it didn't turn out any worse than it was.

Anyway, 1955 was terrible. Trujillo celebrated his 25 years in power with an event he called "The Free World Fair of Peace and Fraternity"—and all the other dictatorships of the moment sent representatives in support of his great reign. This was a time of economic crisis, as I say, and large numbers of Dominicans were leaving the country in search of work. Protest increased among the students and young people. The sons and daughters of the middle class, particularly those from the intellectual families, openly began to reject the regime their parents had supported.

"I belong to a generation that assumed as one of its principal goals the defeat of the dictatorship."

So I belong to a generation that assumed as one of its principal goals the defeat of the dictatorship. In that struggle a great deal of blood was shed, many lives were lost, many dear friends. So much creativity. In 1959 an expedition of young revolutionaries came ashore, supported by the recently victorious Cuban revolution. Some two hundred and fifty men took part in that landing, most of them Dominicans but also including Venezuelans, Puerto Ricans, and Cubans.

For me, for many of my generation, the Cuban revolution was something extraordinary. We hung on its every moment. I want to tell you a story. Trujillo's secret police drove Volkswagens. People were quick to baptize these cars "scrapers," after a kind of scraper used to rasp blocks of ice and make snow cones; you know what I mean: people here call them *frío-fríos*, very-colds. They're popular in the neighborhoods; a guy comes along with his cart, scrapes off the ice, and sprinkles it with syrup.

So the SIM, *Servicio de Inteligencia Militar* (Military Intelligence Service) used these "scrapers." Since the cars circulated at a very slow speed, watching everything, their motors made a familiar sound. For everyone in the Dominican Republic, and especially for those of us who were against the dictatorship, this sound served as a warning…and struck a note of fear. People said that the secret police had special short wave radios and that they could tell if you were listening to foreign stations.

I remember, during the last months of 1958 my father and I listened to Radio Rebelde.[6] We hid in a closet that he'd insulated with a mattress in case it was true that the SIM could really tell if we were listening to a clandestine station. That was how I heard Fidel Castro's first speech after he took power. Hundreds or thousands of young Dominicans like me were inspired by his words, and like me vowed that one day our own country would also be free. We promised ourselves that one day our city would once again be called Santo Domingo.

But, the expedition that arrived on June 14, 1959 ended in a massacre. The resistance movement inside the country and those who had gone into exile never managed to coordinate as they should have. They were no match for the strength of Trujillo's army. In fact, in some of the rural areas it was the farmers themselves who turned the revolutionaries in to the forces of law and order.

Still, the death of those young people wasn't to be in vain. I remember how we all felt when the government publicized that landing. They called it an invasion. And one by one they published the names of the dead. A radio announcer with a very solemn voice would read each name and then say: "Dead."

Trujillo couldn't have imagined the impact this would have on the Dominican people. Every few names there was someone we knew. My father realized that the son of some friends of his, a boy he'd been told was studying outside the country, had really been in exile. Trujillo tried to make all those parents negate the glory of their sons. After June 14, 1959 nothing was ever the same again. And many of us realized that the dictatorship's days were numbered. Before he died, though, he still had some terrible times in store for us all.

Of course the repression strengthened the resistance movement. The university—the only university in the country at that time—had a student population of about 1,500. You had to be privileged to get a higher education, much less to be able to graduate. The revolutionary cells multiplied among those students and among the young professionals. The members of one cell didn't know of the others' existence. And it was in one of those cells, where one of my best friends who was also my cousin was, that we managed to continue the work we'd been doing. That was how I joined the June 14th Movement.

But in January, 1960, Trujillo's forces discovered the network. The first members were picked up on January 21st. And then, like a thread unravelling from a piece of cloth, hundreds and hundreds of people went to jail. In four days three thousand prisoners were counted. I'm talking about a country that at that time couldn't have had more than three million inhabitants. Three thousand prisoners in four days, that's a lot. And what was more startling was that most of these prisoners were sons and daughters of the "good" families: intellectuals, the bourgeoisie, members of the aristocracy that had lost some of its wealth. A number were people who worked for the government itself.

Many of the prisoners were tortured and died, among them my Uncle Manuel. I remembered him singing to me as a child. And he was the one who lit my revolutionary fire. It was he who taught me about democracy, and what an egalitarian distribution of the nation's riches might look like.

"My mother decided to stay in Puerto Rico."

Those were difficult months. My mother decided to stay on in Puerto Rico. When she received word that one of her cousins had died in the June 14th expedition and that returning might pose a problem, she decided to stay. And that's when my mother started trying to get us out of the country as well. She succeeded in November, 1960; when the Dominican government finally allowed us to use the visas the U.S. government had issued. Only my father was not permitted to leave.

So in November of 1960 we children joined our mother after almost a year's separation. Our anguish was having to leave our father behind. Those were critical months in terms of my political education. I was just beginning my last year of high school, and I had developed a wonderful relationship with one of my professors, a Dominican Father who was also critical of the regime. I remember that the nuns were suspicious of our friendship; they'd ask me: "But Magaly, why do you confess so often these days?" Of course I wasn't confessing. Three times a week this Father and I used the confessional booth to coordinate political information that was current in the streets at that time.

Later this "confessor" of mine was also forced into exile, when the Catholic Church publicly called the dictatorship to task. Up to then, the Church had said nothing about the abuses committed in the country. But it reached a point where it could no longer remain silent. That's when the dictatorship turned against the Church.

But for me the decision to leave my country felt like treason. It was as if I was betraying my comrades in struggle. Rarely have I felt as impotent as I did at that moment. There was nothing I could do of course because I was still legally a minor; when my mother sent for me I had to go. As the time of my departure got closer and closer, I felt as if the earth was disintegrating beneath my feet. I suffered the impending loss of my school, the nuns, my friends and their families. I felt like I was losing a part of myself.

In any case, I was forced to leave. And in that rupture I also lost the library I'd so carefully built up over all those years. I gave that library to my school. The same was true of my collection of paper dolls; although it had been a couple of years since I'd played with them I had hundreds of paper dolls all organized in boxes—with their carnival costumes, their party dresses, their sportswear. Imagine, until I was almost fourteen I spent hours playing with those dolls! I'd play with paper dolls and I'd read.

Our arrival in Puerto Rico marked a definite break with my life to that point. It was almost as if I'd emerged anew from my mother's womb. Behind I'd left all that had conformed my nurturing shell, although of course I believed I'd possessed a measure of autonomy. I did my last year of high school in a new place, again with nuns. But these nuns were less flexible. And I was no longer the little girl who had grown up among the nuns of my childhood. I felt out of place among these new sisters, with their unfamiliar habits; and I began to see them as distant and cold. I found all sorts of fault with them. Perhaps my old nuns had the same faults, but I didn't think so.

All of this set the stage for my confrontation with the Catholic Church. The first Sunday we went to mass I remember the priest launched a diatribe against the Cuban revolution. I couldn't believe what I was hearing: how could anyone speak ill of a process that had liberated an entire country? And it wasn't just that he spoke ill. He was establishing the parameters for the whole reactionary campaign against the Cuban revolution, and against the young Cubans who made it.

I was shocked. And of course I had to speak of my feelings to my new confessor. And I was even more shocked when he explained that those Cubans were Communists, that we had to nip Communism in the bud and with everything in our power. I didn't really know what Communism was. Trujillo used the word as an epithet for anyone who happened to be against him. So I didn't put much stock in what the priest told me; he didn't have much credibility with me in any case. For the first time in my life, the Church seemed less than infallible.

This process of disassociation wouldn't be easy though. A book that helped me a great deal was *Listen, Yankee!* by C. Wright Mills. It gave me the arguments I needed to decipher the U.S. government's early acts of hostility against the Cuban revolution. My disengagement with the Church—which came as much from my experience in that new school as it did from my experience in the parish itself—opened me to other ways of thinking.

At the time my mother had managed to take over a boarding house. She ran the place, renting rooms to single men and also offering lunch to those who worked near where we lived, in the neighboring banks and offices. We lived at Tetuán 311, in old San Juan. This was before old San Juan became what it is today—or what they tell me it is today: a bustle of condos and modern buildings. In those days it was the pulsing center of old Puerto Rico, a tourist zone with old colonial houses that had been restored.

My mother built that boarding house into a prosperous business. By the beginning of 1961, an average of 75 people, most of them young men who worked in those nearby offices, had lunch there every day. The food was famous. And the rooms were always full. This was a new experience for me too. Because in Santo Domingo male and female space had been very delineated, very separate. I had gone to an all-girl school, I rarely played with boys, and my own brothers were much older than I was. Even when I played with my male cousins, which was allowed, we were constantly observed by our parents.

All of a sudden I found myself in a world of men, of men who came and went, who spoke their minds, who talked about all sorts of things. And who also listened to me. In the boarding house I met my first political exiles, and I'd listen to them talk about the dictatorship, the things they'd been through, the things that were happening. Stories that shocked even me, because they were beyond what we'd heard on the streets back home. It was also there that one night I went to the room of one of the boarders, a lawyer I remember as a very cultured man, and borrowed a book—a book he'd shown me once before and I'd rejected—*The Communist Manifesto*.

So Puerto Rico taught me a great deal politically. But, what about the people? That was a moment of economic prosperity on the island; it was a kind of showcase for U.S. enterprise, with its prosperous facade, its growing "wealth." And it was a colony of the United States. The majority of Puerto Ricans seemed satisfied with their status of "free association." Those same people rejected words like republic, because to them republic was synonymous with the problems of a dictatorship. They seemed proud of their relationship with the United States.

In my nationalist vision, a vision based in the concepts of autonomy and independence and democracy, the Puerto Rican condition seemed utterly reproachable. I remember experiencing feelings of rage. I'd stand on the balcony of our home and ask myself: "What am I doing here? What am I doing in a country where people don't even respect their own flag, where living well seems to be the most palpable goal?" I felt like a stranger.

Only when I started university—when the Trujillo dictatorship fell in 1961—did I discover Puerto Rico's other face, the face of those struggling for political independence. That was the Puerto Rico that loved its flag, that loved its culture, its language, its music…and I felt I had found my brothers and sisters. Almost immediately I found my place in the FUPI, the Federation of Pro Independence University Students. And so I agreed with my parents' decision not to return to the Dominican Republic—even though the dictatorship had been defeated—but that my father should join us in Puerto Rico. We wouldn't go home until I'd finished my studies.

We did visit our country in the summers, and at Christmas. And we delighted in the bits and pieces of democracy that were beginning to emerge. But I committed myself heart and soul to the Puerto Rican independence movement. My time in college was divided between my responsibilities as a student and my responsibilities as a political cadre. It was my good fortune that being a revolutionary in Puerto Rico in those days not only obliged one to struggle, it also meant a profound study of social change. I was privileged to live my college days among some wonderful revolutionary men and women. My education didn't just include the study of Marxism; it included seeing the latest independent films, listening to the Beatles, reading poetry, and so forth.

It was then that I began to read Latin American poetry, a poetry that I'd never really known before. I read César Vallejo, Pablo Neruda, and I fell in love for life with the Spanish poet Miguel Hernández. He became a favorite, and when I'd travel to Santo Domingo I'd share him with my friends there as well.

Although I participated in the Student Federation, in fact became a member of its leadership of those years, the idea of returning to the Dominican Republic was always present in me. I think for that reason I never allowed myself to fall in love with any of the young men in the Puerto Rican movement. I became involved with men who were not native Puerto Ricans, and I became involved conspicuously late; perhaps as a way of making sure that I wouldn't marry and remain outside my country. Instinctively I knew that would be my destiny—it was the destiny of any young woman at the time—if I allowed myself to fall in love where I was.

"Upon returning home, one of my first acts was to join the June 14th Movement."

During my university career I took regular summer courses, and did everything else within my power to graduate in short order and be able to return to the Dominican Republic. I was able to graduate a semester early, and then my family began to make plans to go home. My mother went first. She rented a house while I stayed behind to take my last exams. By December 23, 1964 I was back in Santo Domingo. My goal was to find work and then return briefly to San Juan in order to graduate with my class.

Upon returning home, one of my first acts was to join the June 14th Movement, an organization that had become a political party when the masses of prisoners were released at the end of the dictatorship. I'd already made contact with many of its leaders when I'd returned during vacations in '62, '63, and in the summer of '64—when my sister was married. By this time my cousin was a leader of one of the more radical left groups, but I'd remained close to the June 14th Movement, particularly to its student wing.

When I came home and began working with the Party's propaganda arm, we were underground. Juan Bosch[7] had been elected president in 1962, but the following year he'd been over-thrown by a military coup—aided of course by the United States, by the most conservative elements in the country, and by the Church. At that point our movement was forced into clan-destinity. Most of the opposition parties were declared illegal and had to continue their work under those conditions.

Those of us who weren't marked were able to remain above ground for a time; we worked in the information and pro-paganda brigades. One night, walking along the city's sea wall, the person who had brought me into party ranks introduced me to "Raul," the name used for many years by the man who would later become my husband. He'd been in exile in Cuba for many months. Now he was back in the Dominican Republic and headed one of the propaganda units. Today one of our grand-children is named Raul.

It was also during that early political militancy that I expe-rienced my first cultural clashes. You know, Puerto Rican society was more cosmopolitan in many ways, with more of a liberal influence, modeled after the United States. I had gotten used to going out by myself, to going to the movies or dancing with a group of friends, without someone coming along to watch over me—a chaperon, if you will. My mother, too, had always trust-ed me to be out on my own.

So when I returned to Santo Domingo that independence of mine clashed with prevailing customs. Customs on the part of the women as well as of the men. I remember my contempo-raries assuming that since I was used to going out by myself I also must be freer with my sexuality. Our revolutionary youth, many of them came from the Christian movement. That was the case with Fafa, my husband, who had been an altar boy as a child and who'd tried to enter a seminary but wasn't accepted because his parents had been married by civil law and not in the Church. All these pure, idealistic revolutionaries had a great many problems when it came to normal human relations.

They all had their girlfriends. But their girlfriends never went out alone. And they wouldn't have thought of having premarital relations. So it's been up to us, the women, not only to take our places in the transformation of society but to figure out how to change the inequality in the relationships between our brothers and ourselves.

"I began to deconstruct—and construct—myself."

This was an important time in my life, as it was in the life of my country. During these years I was part of the active resistance movement. And I married a man who was also deeply involved in that movement. I began to have our children…and there was Fafa's time underground, followed by his imprisonment.

My comrade seemed to possess a very complete concept of social change. I, perhaps because of my experience in Puerto Rico, remained somewhat skeptical. But one day, a journalist from the United States, a man who worked for one of the alternative news agancies and was covering Balaguer's reelection in 1970—the man's still a good friend of mine—sent me a small book with a fuchsia cover. It was the anthology you edited, Margaret, of writings from the early feminist movement. My friend had found the book in Mexico. That was my first contact with the women's liberation movement.[8]

I'll never forget the emotion with which I read that little book, and the effect some of the essays produced in me. The one that really changed me was Juliette Mitchell's "Women: The Longest Revolution." I suppose it was only logical; it was a Marxist analysis, and with my particular training and experience those would be the words I'd hear most clearly. But I also remember Naomi Weisstein's essay;[9] she explored the psychology of women, their relationships. It was more of an experience piece. And it gave me the language to speak of some of what had been bothering me.

That little book of yours was like a life preserver thrown to a drowning swimmer. I read it again and again; I read some parts so many times that I actually learned them by heart! And I began trying to put some of what I learned into practice, in the work I was already doing with women through my political militancy. Because after the fall of the dictator and before our big defeat in 1965, we were able to create a number of above-ground organizations; public groupings of women which, perhaps because of the very sexism of Latin American men, proved more difficult to destroy.

Central among these organizations was the Federation of Dominican Women.[10] I was involved in the Federation, and I worked with the women; although it was always a rather limited type of work: our motto was "Shoulder to Shoulder with Our Men," that type of thing. The old idea of women in the supporting role, linking women's liberation to the struggle to build a new society.

Eventually that work in the Federation paled, because internal factionalism gained the upper hand. But I still had an ardent desire to work with women. And your book gave me the theory I needed to plan a much more systematic type of work. It also opened me to other readings: Alexandra Kollontai,[11] for example, and Flora Tristán.[12] And Wilhelm Reich,[13] whose theories about young people and sexuality were so important. Reich saw sexual oppression as one of the pivotal points of state-imposed control.

So, armed with these four or five books—but mainly with Juliette Mitchell's article—I launched my first campaign among the women. And it wasn't to be a subtle campaign. That is to say, it wasn't by any means a gradual process. I was undoubtedly ready for this. I'd been working with women, as I say, and I already had a lot of questions, product of the particular methodologies we'd been using in the Party, the lack of answers in this area, and the vacuum created by the total failure of interpretation in the classic Marxist texts. Almost immediately I became a passionate feminist. And I began to speak of feminism.

When I think back to those times, I want to laugh. I call it my sharpshooter period. There wasn't a comment, an incident, an event, that I didn't counter with my analysis. I explained patriarchy and denounced sexism wherever I found it. My friends said: "We can't even joke around you!" And I myself became the butt of many jokes; no sooner than I'd show up, the conversation would invariably turn to that passion of mine: women's condition and women's rights. Actually, that was a very interesting time in my life. And it was an interesting process. Because as I constructed my theoretical framework, I began to deconstruct—and construct—myself.

"Our goal was a truly Dominican feminism."

This of course included an analysis of my life with my husband. And it came at a time when my husband was in prison.[14] There's an interesting story here: political literature wasn't allowed into the prison then, but feminist literature wasn't considered political. So my comrade was able to accompany me on my journey through this literature. And of course that gave rise to a good many discussions, and no few confrontations.

And then I was involved with a group of women around 1973, Women's Promotion I think we called ourselves, and that was the first group in our country that put out a frankly feminist analysis. We sponsored a seminar on abortion;[15] from today's perspective I don't know where we found the courage, or why we weren't lynched back then for that! And when Women's Promotion disappeared I asked myself why we hadn't been able to create a feminist movement with political power. Why we weren't able to mobilize women and use our strength to create political pressure, like women in the industrialized countries were beginning to do.

The analysis took me a while. But I began to realize that we middle-class women, those most socially like our sisters in the United States, had one significant difference. And this was that you women in the States—students, professionals, young married women, whatever your position—most of you had to carry a domestic load as you struggled in your area of study or of work. That is, your insertion into the labor force and the salaries you earned from that work didn't free you from domesticity, they didn't really free you. (We weren't even talking about the double shift back then.) What I saw was that your daily practice generated an awakening regarding women's oppression; you clearly saw the social division of labor and how women were oppressed in the private sphere.

I saw you demanding of your male counterparts that they do their share in the home. And your discussions had implications, like whether or not to have children, whether or not you could stay in school, whether or not you could even work outside the home. You were radicalized through this sort of discussion and the options that did or didn't exist. This radicalization on the part of middle-class women in the United States produced the movement we witnessed. And even many housewives, although they didn't have the pressure of a double shift, were drawn in because of their generally high educational levels. Because they began to question the emptiness of their lives.

But we women in the Dominican Republic didn't have either of these situations. Among our middle-class and upper-middle-class women it began to be fashionable to get an education and go to work in one of the professions. But we didn't have so much trouble juggling our traditional roles because in our culture we all had maids who cleaned our houses, cooked our family's meals, washed and ironed the clothes and so forth. Domestic service was so poorly paid that even a woman without a particularly high income had one or two women working in her home. We didn't suffer the same sort of tensions in this area as you did.

This situation, not only in the Dominican Republic but throughout Latin America, meant that while numbers of middle-class or professional women assumed feminism in theory, very few of us really lived the tensions in our daily lives. Feminism didn't become a real part of our political project. On the other hand, our housewives remained at home precisely because they had never had access to the levels of education that would have allowed them to become more independent through their contact with the outside world.

What we had was a housewife with little formal education for whom our arguments didn't seem that relevant. Let's take the issue of autonomy that the women's movement was dealing with then. Most of our middle-class or lower-middle-class housewives were more interested in keeping a husband who would bring in a salary than they were in talking about their own autonomy. A husband meant an income, he meant a certain status, and in some neighborhoods he was even required in terms of personal security. We had a problem on our hands: how to talk about women's rights among our popular sectors, how to talk about our rights even among the middle class and intellectuals? After many forums and discussions, after attending the 1975 non-governmental forum on women's rights in Mexico[16], I was able to read more, to consider other studies and theories—the fact that I was able to read in English was important to all this— and I began to formulate my own theory of popular feminism.

We presented what I call popular feminism for the first time at a seminar in Santo Domingo in 1978. I worked on this with several other Dominican women. Our goal was to develop a truly Dominican feminism, something that would work for us. We wanted to work among the large masses of women in our country. "Towards a Popularly-Based Feminism" was my first attempt in this regard, and it was a work that received its share of criticism from some of the South American feminists at one of the first theoretical meetings I attended, in Rio de Janeiro in 1982. That's where I met women like Virginia Vargas, Julieta Kirkwood, etc. They listened to me respectfully, but weren't really willing to call what I was saying feminist.

At the same time, I was looking for ways to put my ideas into practice. The Brazilian Moema Viezzer, the woman who wrote that well-known book of testimony, *Let Me Speak,*[17] was spending some time in the Dominican Republic. I became familiar with her methodology, and through her I also came in contact with Paolo Freire and his ideas about grass-roots education. These contacts moved me to found an institution to work with women, in three basic areas: education, research, and the development of methodologies that would help us in our work. I knew I needed this in order to strengthen the feminist work I wanted to do with women in the popular sectors.

This, in 1980, is how CIPAF was born. To begin with I called on some twenty women, to talk about my idea. But we didn't get anywhere. There was a great deal of fragmentation on the Left at that time. The different groups were riddled with ideological differences. So it ended up being three of us who started CIPAF. One was Thelma Gálvez, a Chilean woman who lived in Santo Domingo with her husband who was a diplomat. She was thinking about going back home at the time. Another was Quintina Reyes, a Puerto Rican woman who also lived in our country. Our first initiative was to make contact with someone we'd met from Holland, to try to get funding. We needed office space, a place of our own. While this was in process, I went to Nicaragua. And that trip would also mark an important turning point in my life. I'd been working for several years in solidarity with the Sandinistas, but by 1979 that work had become more intense because of the presence in our country of a political exile named Javier Chamorro. He and his family gave a tremendous push to our solidarity movement. By the time the Sandinistas won their war I was solidly committed to their cause. Almost immediately—I think it was in September or October of 1979—I made my first trip.

"Nicaragua...for the first time in many years, I had a room of my own."

Of course I made immediate contact with the women in Nicaragua, with the Sandinista women. And that led to my going to work for a time in one of the newly-created ministries, the Ministry of Social Welfare. That was the first ministry in Nicaragua headed by a woman, Lea Guido. And it was set up to deal with women's issues. In February of 1980, and as part of an agreement between the university in Santo Domingo—where I'd been working—and the Sandinista government, I went to work in Nicaragua. I was there through July of the same year, working at the Ministry of Social Welfare. I helped design what would later become the Nicaraguan Women's Office.

That experience gave me a lot. For one thing, for the first time in many years I had "a room of my own." This time without children as well. It was fantastic. After all those years of attending to the needs of others, I could get up in the morning, go to work at the Ministry, and then that night I could decide to stay over at Ana's if I wanted to, or at Norma's, wherever I happened to be. I could stay over with Milú. I wasn't inundated with domestic tasks; I didn't have to take a child to the dentist, oversee another's homework, or deal with household bills, nothing like that.

I should say that I had a baby at the time; she was born in 1978. She came about as a result of Fafa's release from prison. Our agreement was that he would be the main person responsible for that child's care, since I had been the "single parent" with our two previous children. So he stayed home with the two older children and our little girl who was then just a year and a half, and I went off on my Nicaraguan adventure. It was to be one of the most important times of my life. Those were moments of tremendous creativity, sharing with the Sandinistas who had survived long years of dictatorship and were just beginning to develop the social structures that would give them a new life.

It was important for me to see how those men and women who had lived for so long in conditions of clandestinity were able to adapt to their new situation. And I met many extraordinary women especially, marvelous marvelous women. Many people come away impressed by the fact that so many Nicaraguans are poets, and of course many of the women are poets. I continue to be incredibly impressed by the strength, the power, the tenderness, the initiative, and the will of those beautiful Nicaraguan women.

The friendships I made during those months in Nicaragua have continued to grow over the years, and I've returned to

Nicaragua many times, sharing their difficulties as well as their joys. I feel that Nicaragua is a second homeland. When you ask me, Margaret, if I feel Latin American or simply Dominican, I can truthfully say that I'm a Dominican who feels deeply indebted to Puerto Rico and who loves Nicaragua profoundly as well. Almost all my Nicaraguan women friends, for instance, love to dance the Merengue. And they dance it well. We've danced together.

"I used to tell them: 'Look, Lenin wasn't born here...neither did the Pope grow up in my neighborhood!'"

Anyway, when I returned to Santo Domingo, we had the funding we needed to start CIPAF. Its first home was a small office at The New School,[18] which was already seven years old by then and had its own building. We started with a great deal of enthusiasm, a lot of creativity, and very clear goals. One of these was a research line, through which we wanted to make women's social contributions more visible and legitimize their efforts. I knew this was important, so that our society in general would come to understand that when we spoke of women's oppression it wasn't an empty term.

We had to get people to see what discrimination against women was, what shape it took, and how that discrimination held our whole society back. Our research projects also helped us publicize important feminist issues. For example, the issue of domestic violence, violence against women, sexual violence. These were things that hadn't been articulated in our country, and when you tried to talk about them people accused you of importing U.S. issues into a reality where they weren't important.

That's always the case, of course, when you put forth new political ideas; there are always those who hide behind a facade of false nationalism in order to defend themselves. When we spoke out as feminists, the Left as well as the Right accused us of importing foreign ideas, strange ideas that were popular among women in the so-called developed countries. You'd hear this sort of thing from anyone, from a Catholic who based his ideas on someone like Saint Augustine—hardly a native son!—to a Marxist whose ideology came from just as far afield. I used to tell them: "Look, Lenin wasn't born here...neither did the Pope grow up in my neighborhood! Your political theory or your religious ideas are as foreign as my feminism is."

So it was pretty difficult. There were only a few of us who were willing to call ourselves feminists back then. And we were frequent objects of attack. It was also hard to maintain a continuity in the work, because we weren't all that theoretically advanced. Nevertheless it was a comfort belonging to a group of some sort, a collective effort.

Before CIPAF would put a new issue out there—open to ridicule—we'd make sure we'd undertaken a study. For example, in spite of the fact that our country thought of itself as a safe haven, we knew that every thirteen hours a rape was reported to the police. Our mass media only publicized about ten percent of these rapes. It cost us a great deal to bring attention to this situation; lots of people said what we were really trying to do was to divide the poor, or to divide the working class. Now, many years later and after all our work, we can see that the issues of domestic violence and sexual assault are accepted parts of the social agenda in our country. Many other voices have joined ours in demanding channels and mechanisms through which to deal with these problems. People are asking for better systems of protection and stiffer punishment for the perpetrators.

I think one of the most positive aspects of our work has been this: that each time we've introduced a new theme we've been able to support our point of view with studies of our own reality. In this way we've dealt with issues like abortion and prostitution, we've done studies on the lives of rural women and researched the situation of the women who work in the free trade zones.

Another of our lines of work is educational. We've used our studies to produce materials which we give back to the women themselves, so that they may become subjects in their own process of consciousness raising, around the issues that affect them most. We want to help them move from an individual awareness to a collective social consciousness. This area of work is very important to us. At CIPAF, from the beginning we've done this type of seminar with rural women as well as women who work in the factories. We also go into the poorest neighborhoods, here in Santo Domingo. And in recent years we've been able to move into other sectors as well. Recently I think we've made another qualitative leap; without neglecting our work with all these women, we've gained a larger space in the media, a way of influencing a broader range of public opinion.

Like someone said to me the other day, it's not hip anymore for a man to say he's *macho*. And that used to be a source of masculine pride here. I'm not saying this makes men any less sexist, just that they're not willing to publicly identify themselves that way. It's all part of the work we're doing. There are some seven and a half million Dominicans at this point in time, and we have nine TV channels, ten national newspapers, 240 radio stations. People are accustomed to listening in, taking part in a variety of debates, and sexism—or *machismo*, as we call it here—is a frequent subject of popular discussion.

Our presence is making itself felt. And also in areas that are difficult to measure at this point, like among the teachers. We have a project in coordination with our Ministry of Education, through which we're trying to achieve non-sexist sex education in the schools. We feel that one of our priority tasks is to enable our young people to go through a process of positive socialization from the earliest age. So we've put a lot of energy into this work we're doing with teachers.

Another one of our lines is advocating for more political power for women, not only for more rights but so we can exert a greater influence in our society. Since 1986 we've been working steadily with women in the different political parties. We want those parties to include women's rights in their programmatic platforms. And I think we've made progress here. The parties not only recognize that women constitute an electoral force, and try to win our vote; I think they also take our demands more seriously.

CIPAF is involved in generating and maintaining relations with other parts of the women's movement. Living on an island inevitably leads to an isolation of sorts. We often hear things like: "Nobody stops here…nobody takes us into account." For the islander there are two possibilities: you can either remain engrossed in your own reality or you can connect with those beyond your borders. Maybe that's why there's been such an enormous Dominican emigration, a diaspora that goes from the United States—where more than 700,000 Dominicans live—to our women who go to Spain to work as maids, or as prostitutes in Greece and Italy, Germany, Switzerland, even some of the Arab nations.

From the very beginning, CIPAF has put a lot of energy into nurturing our ties with the international women's movement. We started by building on the links I'd established in Mexico in 1975—International Year of the Woman—and which I expanded in 1980 at the conference in Copenhagen. We started publishing a bulletin in which we could share our experiences. And through the years we've built a documentation center where at the moment we have more than 11,000 items from all over the world. We receive information from Latin America especially, and our publication goes out to 1,500 organizations and individuals.

We've also had visits from the most interesting Latin American feminists; they come to do workshops or lectures, and when they can't come they send their books. There's a lot of interest here. In fact, the Dominican delegation was the largest to attend the meeting of feminists from Latin America and the Caribbean that took place in Bogotá in 1981. Two hundred sixty women attended. There have been five meetings since then, and 5,000 and 2,000 women were at the last two. That first was a very important meeting for us. And I'm happy to say that the great majority of those of us who were in that delegation continues to be active in feminist work here at home; some of us running non-governmental organizations, some of us writing or teaching, each in her particular niche.

Back when I began talking about a broad-based feminism, I couldn't have dreamt of the movement we have here today. I think I can say that in the Dominican Republic feminism has permeated every area of women's life. Certainly many women don't call themselves feminists, but even these women—in one way or another—claim the issues we've put forth. You can see this in groups of rural women all the way up to groups of female executives. And you can see it among the women active in the different political parties.

The Dominican feminist movement may not be able to rally a large public meeting or a march, but its presence can be felt in all areas of society. People have to take us and our ideas into account. And they know the force we can generate through public opinion. I think we've gained our space as a social movement.

We have different faces, of course. Because one thing we've learned is that a single woman's organization, like the one we had here with our Federation of Dominican Women, isn't viable. We need many different expressions of our multiple identities: as women of different races and ethnicities, different classes, different generations, as well as a diversity of interests.

We have women working in public health, in education, with groups of women in the trades or the professions, with women who are looking for ways to earn a living, in research projects, at the universities; in other words, our movement has a variety of expressions.

You ask about a lesbian movement here. We've had two lesbian collectives, and one of them still exists. But these haven't had much of a public presence. Some of the members are well-known, of course, and from time to time they've issued proclamations of one kind or another, or denounced particular situations. But that's as far as it's gone. I have a feeling there isn't going to be an "out" lesbian movement as such for a while; the nature of our society makes it very difficult. On the other hand —and I think this is very important—some of the most visible lesbians are among the respected intellectuals of our women's movement. And among the younger women they represent a solid up-and-coming strength.

I know you're interested in the links we've been able to make with the feminist movements in Central America. Besides my connection with Nicaragua—which I've already gone into— in recent years I've worked closely with the other Central American movements. I've been in touch with women in Panama, Guatemala, Honduras; trying to strengthen the Latin American movement in general.

Latin American feminism has its own face. I don't think we've produced all that much original theory yet, but we've been able to develop very innovative and creative methodologies that have greatly aided in raising consciousness in our countries. This has helped make feminism a mass movement. And I think it's precisely this that's been our greatest contribution. It's not the same as the more theoretical advances made in the industrialized countries. But it's enabled us to introduce feminist ideas into a variety of discourses and practices.

For example we have women in the countryside, women farmworkers, women in the free trade zones and in the professions, all with their own particular feminist discourse. Therein lies a great deal of our strength, in our ability to penetrate so many different areas and acquaint many different types of women with our ideas. Feminism for us is a mass phenomenon.

"We feminists aren't afraid of menopause."

Margaret, I turned fifty last year. And I was thinking of having a great party to celebrate. I'd had a huge party when I was forty, with a banner proclaiming the fact that "We Feminists Aren't Afraid of Menopause." We aren't afraid of admitting our age. I confess that at fifty I wasn't quite so out there with my proclamations…. I was feeling a bit less casual about the processes I was experiencing. Still, I wanted to have a big party. And I wanted to emphasize the fact that we can and must grow older free of the stigmas society places upon us.

Unfortunately—and it's become somewhat commonplace among those of my generation—I lost my father a few days before my birthday. During the preceding couple of years we'd gotten particularly close. My mother and father had divorced after many years of marriage, and my father lived alone. (I forgot to mention that they were divorced following that time in Puerto Rico, when my mother managed to attain her own autonomy—with the boarding house and all that. She no longer felt she had to take all my father dished out. And I suddenly discovered the flip side of a marriage I'd always assumed was idyllic. My mother showed me that other side: my father's infidelities, his hostilities and so forth. It was an important lesson, an important moment in my life. I lost my illusions about my father, but I gained a new relationship with my mother—who continues to be a dynamic woman at the age of 78.)

In all that I'd distanced myself from my father to some extent. But during the last two years of his life, when he began to feel his age—he was 89 when he died—we became quite close once more. We had some important times together. I realize that my father taught me to love the smallest things in life, and that I used that lesson to great advantage during the most difficult years, when I was out of work or was only able to get poorly paid jobs. He and my mother also gave me a very happy childhood. They really loved me well when I was small; I can look through a family photo album and remember so many happy times, that it's helped me through the worst of times, enabling me to go on.

So when I turned fifty I didn't have a party after all. But at CIPAF we produced a special issue of *Quehaceres* (Tasks). A group of feminists of my generation celebrated this new age we've come to, these new experiences in our lives. I have grandchildren now: my oldest daughter married young and I have a grandchild who's seven. And another who's two and a half. They don't live near us, they're in Toronto. But we see each other whenever we can and we talk a lot on the phone.

My son Rafael Francisco, who's 27, is married to a wonderful woman who worked with us at CIPAF for a while. She's currently expecting their first child. We're all hoping it will be a girl of course! And my mother is overjoyed at being a grandmother and a great-grandmother. The role our society demanded of grandmothers in times gone by, that of being present at the birth, of physically helping with that rite of passage: my mother assumes that role with her great-grandchildren. Because this grandmother—me, the feminist grandmother—is still too involved in her work to be able to get away and take that responsibility on, spend months caring for a grandchild or helping its mother give birth. Maybe I'll be doing that for my great-grandchildren, I don't know. If I end up living as long as my grandmother, who died when she was 97, maybe I'll be able to experience the joy of knowing my own great-grandchildren.

"My daughter also had to find her own ways to rebel against me."

You ask about generational differences. My oldest daughter Syra grew up in a feminist household, with very definite ideas regarding a non-sexist education. During her adolescence she and I had some pretty tough confrontations. My rebellion had seemed just; after all, my generation had to break with the generation that put the dictator in office. But my daughter also had to find her own ways to rebel against me. I spoke with her honestly. I offered her sex education from an early age. And so she was forced to work out her rebellion by demanding the right to use makeup or dress in a way that we feminists of the '70s considered representative of the consumer society, sexually objectifying.

For what seemed like a long time my daughter asserted herself by taking the opposite position on everything we '70s feminists believed in. They called us "clean-faced feminists" because we didn't use makeup. We dressed like hippies, wore sandals. So my daughter learned early to primp and sport the fashions of the times. Today she's an executive in the tourism industry. She's very beautiful, with great taste, and I think she's been able to assimilate the most important of the lessons I've tried to pass on. She's a very strong woman. I know she's gotten that from me. And in spite of the fact that she dresses well and enjoys it, she's never let that get in the way of making her own way in life, going after what she wants and achieving it. For me it's been interesting to have a daughter who's not only a successful business woman, but a prosperous one as well.

We still have Marcelle at home, her full name is Marcelle Victoria Paloma. She's got three names because we never managed to settle on one that I liked, or my kids or my husband liked. Very democratically we burdened the poor girl with three. She's fifteen now. Her father calls her his daughter; that is, the two oldest are mine and she's "his." But in spite of the fact that he's the one who's spent the most time with her, she and I get on magnificently. Often we stand together against some opinion of his, in one or another of the many debates that go on within a family. Marcelle is in junior high school. And I, who wasn't so sure in 1978 that we should be having a third child, am very happy that we did.

"From the tip of Chile to a tiny island in the Caribbean...we see women rising up."

Your last question asks what I'd want to say to U.S. readers of a book like this one. That's hard. Let's see.... Maybe I should go back to the question about establishing links and how our movement has changed over the last two decades. I remember something I've been saying for a while: although the economists insist that the decade of the '80s was a time of loss for Latin America, I believe that for women, especially Latin American women, it was a time of great gain. In spite of the economic crisis. In spite of having to tighten our belts. In spite of our struggle to survive.

In almost all our countries women have made extraordinary strides in education. And I think this has been important in terms of our recognizing our own dependency, recognizing the need to fight for our rights, to fight for equality. Women have also moved massively into the labor force during this period of time. And even though this hasn't always signaled the kind of independence we're looking for, or the political involvement we might like, I think it's introduced a different sort of logic into women's way of thinking. It's changed the nature of our relationships.

The immense growth of our women's movements has also been important. It's phenomenal how, from the tip of Chile to a tiny island in the Caribbean, or lately in Mexico with the Zapatistas, we see women rising up. Indigenous women are beginning to make known their demands, like the *mestizas* (mixed bloods) have made ours known, and the professional women. We're seeing movement after movement with women in the forefront. And we've moved from a time of denunciation to a time of action—without giving up denunciation because there's certainly a lot to denounce. But we've gained a great deal of space in the subjective consciousness of our peoples.

I think that the feminist movements in Latin America possess an originality, a creativity, and a force that allow them to speak with authority in the struggle with the North. We've acquired a confidence in ourselves, so that in spite of the terrible disasters, in spite of the corruption of our governments, in spite of our material situation, the debt, the natural disasters we've suffered—the earthquakes, hurricanes, volcanos in eruption and devastating mud slides—in spite of all that constitutes our lives and would seem to rob us of our hope, we women have managed to feel confident. We women especially.

We women cling to hope and continue to put forth the idea that a better world is possible. I think this gives us a solid base from which to talk to women in the United States or in Europe, in places where in a certain sense hope seems to have been lost. Where the material aspects of life may have improved but where values and relationships seem less important. In spite of our lot in life, we continue to sing and dance. And in our song and in our dance we find joy, and proposals for peace.

We have a writer who has achieved a measure of fame in our country: Juan Luis Guerra. He's put words to our contagious music, always dignifying women, dignifying life. I'd like to close this conversation with the title from one of his best-known songs, a Merengue that people all over Latin America sing as an anthem of hope. It goes back to just wanting to sit down with you, and share that "cup of coffee." The song is called "*¡Ojalá que llueva café!*" ("Here's hoping it rains coffee!").

—Summer, 1994

Notes

1. Very minor changes have been made in order to eliminate redundancy and occasionally to clarify a name or term.
2. PRD, *Partido Revolucionario Dominicano* (Dominican Revolutionary Party). Magaly's husband, Rafael-Fafa-Taveras, did win a congressional seat.
3. *Centro de Investigación Para la Acción Femenina* (Research Center for Women's Action), Luis F. Thomén #358, del Ensanche Quisqueya, Santo Domingo, Dominican Republic. Post Office Box #1744. The organization currently has 42 full-time staff.
4. In the Dominican Republic, at that time, girls generally married between the ages of 13 and 18.
5. *El Colegio Serafín de Asís* (Serafín de Asís School).
6. The clandestine Cuban radio transmitting from the Sierra Maestra mountains.
7. Juan Bosch, of left origins, represented the *Partido de la Liberación Dominicana* (PLD, Dominican Liberation Party). It exists today but has moved to a centrist position.
8. *Las mujeres* by Margaret Randall (Mexico City: Siglo XXI, Editores S.A., 1970). By 1986, this book had gone into its ninth edition.
9. "Kinde, Kuche, Kirche as Scientific Law. Psychology Constructs

119

the Woman" by Naomi Weisstein, in *Las Mujeres*.

10. The Federation of Dominican Women was part of the movement that emerged following the Second World War, of an International Federation of Women with chapters in many countries. This movement was sponsored by the Soviet Union, and the federations modeled after the Soviet party's women's federation.

11. Russian revolutionary and feminist, 1873-1952.

12. Upper-class Peruvian woman who traveled to Europe and wrote a book called *Confesiones de una paria* (*Confessions of a Pariah*). She lived in the 19th century, is sometimes referred to as the first feminist socialist of Latin America, and when she died was buried by French workers in their local cemetery.

13. Wilhelm Reich was an Austrian psychoanalyst, born 1897, disciple of Freud's who broke with the master. He was a one time member of the Austrian Communist Party, thrown out because of his theories of sexuality, famous for his theory of orgone energy and less so for his analysis of sexual politics in the young Soviet Union and the ground-breaking and sexually liberating work he did among German workers. Reich left several groups of followers, among them those involved in today's Radix Therapy, a type of body work which has proved useful in working with survivors of childhood abuse. He died in the Federal Penitentiary in Lewisburg, Pennsylvania, in November of 1957, while serving a two-year sentence for having distributed his invention, the orgone energy accumulator.

14. Rafael-Fafa Tavares was in prison from July, 1970 to July, 1975. He was accused of having been the "intellectual author" of the kidnapping of a U.S. embassy military attaché for whom political prisoners were exchanged.

15. Abortion remains illegal in the Dominican Republic. Unsanctioned and unsafe abortions are performed, as they were here during our own period of illegality, endangering the lives of hundreds if not thousands of women.

16. The non-governmental or alternative forum took place at the same time as the official U.N. World Conference on Women.

17. *Let Me Speak! Testimony of Domitila, A Woman of the Bolivian*

Mines, by Domitila Barrios de Chungara with Moema Viezzer, New York City: Monthly Review Press, 1978.

18. Magaly Pineda founded The New School, a private coeducational grade school that made use of advanced educational methods. Although she no longer works there, she remains on its board of directors. It continues to be a very successful educational endeavor in Santo Domingo.

Market woman, Mercado Oriental, Managua

Julia Aguirre, Nicaraguan painter, Managua

Mother of a "disappeared," Managua

North American women paint in solidarity with Nicaragua Children's Library, Managua, 1982. L to R: Marilyn Lindstrom, Miranda Bergman, Yeshi Neumann. This mural was later destroyed by the post-electoral mayor of Managua.

Sandinista high command remembers and reconstructs the taking of León in June, 1979.

4

To Change Our Own Reality and The World

A Conversation with Lesbians in Nicaragua[1]

*

I lived in Nicaragua from late 1979 through early 1984, during the decade of Sandinista government. I was a middle-aged and middle-class white woman from the United States; a mother of four children, two of whom accompanied me to Managua. Through almost two decades in Mexico and then during my years in Cuba, I had been in close touch with political movements to make change possible—for people and, increasingly as I began to understand my own feminism, for women. I had written a number of books of essays and oral history, often dealing with feminist issues. Several of these books focussed on women in Nicaragua.[2] At that time I called myself a socialist and a feminist. Today I am still a socialist, still a feminist, and a lesbian.

At the time of my move to Nicaragua, the FSLN[3] had recently taken power with a mixture of socialist, nationalist, Christian, and indigenous concepts of how to bring about social change— and with enormous energy and a makeshift creativity unique to its particular history and culture. The United States was already doing everything possible to defeat this new experiment; everyone knew it, as the evidence of overt as well as covert warfare surfaced early on. But the mostly young men and women who had waged and won the recent war believed their magic would carry them through. Every problem was being addressed: land, the economy, education, health, housing, recreation and the arts, as well as freedom.

Freedom, to those who had lived through the Somoza years, often meant little more than being able to leave your house in the morning with some sense that you would return that evening alive. Then there was the freedom to learn how to read and write, powerfully addressed by the 1980 literacy crusade. The freedom to own title to the land one worked. The freedom to hold a job, to be healthy and to have healthy children.

A number of gender issues found a receptive ear among the Sandinistas. One of the revolution's first decrees was against the use of women's bodies in commercial advertising. Irresponsible paternity—a man's fathering one or more children and then going off to leave the mother to care for them— was a widespread problem, and the new government established Women's Offices[4] to defend the economic needs of single or abandoned mothers. Fully a third of the victorious Sandinista army was female, and a number of women showed exceptional political and military leadership. We talked about the fact that among the Sandinistas, women struggled for equality in the ranks before taking power, rather than leaving the issue of sexism to be grappled with later.

León, the first city to be liberated completely so that it could house the provisional revolutionary government, had been taken by a woman: Commander Dora María Téllez. Although no women were on the FSLN's nine-member National Directorate, at all succeeding levels women occupied positions of responsibility and power.[5] Still, in that Nicaragua of the early 1980s, abortion was considered too dangerous an issue to tackle, violence against women was not discussed, and lesbian rights didn't even seem to be on the horizon.[6]

From shortly after the Sandinista victory, AMNLAE[7] was Nicaragua's mass women's organization. It was firmly controlled by the FSLN, acquiring and forfeiting degrees of autonomy but never really operating independently of the Front. The question of whether a women's movement not led by women can make real inroads against sexism and women's oppression is still being debated in Nicaragua and elsewhere. AMNLAE defended many women's rights and opened ideological as well as material space in the struggle to better women's lives. But the organization ultimately did more to rally women around the revolution than to make women's issues a revolutionary priority.

For the first time since leaving Nicaragua early in 1984, I returned for a brief visit in October, 1991. It was heartbreaking to see the changes, so typical of the underdevelopment and dependency suffered by the majority of Third World countries. Where before a monthly basket of essential goods—rice, beans, sugar, cooking oil, soap, and other necessities—had been government-subsidized to every family, now the markets were filled but at prices few could afford. Sex education and other progressive programs were no longer a part of public schooling. Headlines screamed of epidemic hospital deaths caused by problems with elemental cleanliness, as well as an extreme shortage of antibiotics and other drugs.

For the most part I found Sandinista political cadre disoriented. The shock of the electoral loss, a year and a half before, lingered in the air like some lethargic cloud. U.S. promises of generous economic aid had not materialized. In the midst of continued economic crisis, the chaos of new political divisions, ex-Contras and ex-Sandinistas in the rural areas renewing armed struggle as *Revueltos*,[8] and repressive legislation rolling back many of the last decade's gains, women now appeared to be the single most vibrant and active political force.

AMNLAE was going through a profound reevaluation of its role. Issues such as abortion (illegal before, during, and since the Sandinista government) and domestic violence, once considered too "feminist," are now the subjects of priority campaigns. But many revolutionary women feel that AMNLAE still fails to address their most important demands. These women are organizing outside what was once the single women's movement. Young women, calling themselves The 52% Majority, celebrated International Women's Day that year with a large public program. Lesbian feminists, claiming these two words in how they speak about themselves, are also beginning to have a multifaceted presence.

Women from some of the more conservative women's groups had crossed political lines to meet with their revolutionary sisters. Shortly after my October visit (in January, 1992), close to 800 women would come together in Managua for an energetic gathering. Peasant women, professionals, women from within and outside of AMNLAE, feminists and lesbian feminists, religious women, and even the only woman to have had a seat on the Contras'high command, all shared experiences and ideas.

It was in this atmosphere—economically impoverished, desperate, shell-shocked, exhausted from years of superhuman work but bursting with questions that could no longer be shelved—that I asked to meet with a group of lesbians willing to speak about their recent history. I wanted to know how their movement had started; it had been quite invisible when I lived in Managua in the early '80s. I wanted to hear about how they conceived of their struggle, the responses they were getting from various quarters, and what their concerns and projects were.

We met on one of those hot wet nights typical of October in Managua. The rainy season. Where a group of women talked with one another in a circle of rattan rockers, the lush leaves of large tropical plants dripped moisture onto the tile floor. Half inside, half out…like so many sitting rooms that become patios and then sitting rooms again in houses half-hidden behind high walls.

These women see themselves as part of a lesbian, gay, and bisexual movement. Many if not most of those involved are Sandinista revolutionaries. Sandinism clearly opened a space for diverse freedoms even when it did not succeed in fully taking up their cause.[9] It's also worth noting that gay and lesbian organizing has been going on throughout Central and South America for the past eight to ten years. Regional gatherings of lesbians have been taking place in places like Mexico, Argentina, and Costa Rica.

Ana, who is a founding member of *Puntos de Encuentro* (Common Ground), a feminist center that works with young men and women, with gays and lesbians, and with women in the broad-based independent women's movement, had been able to contact several of the more active members of the Nicaraguan movement. And so, on this humid night, before some of these women had even come to the end of their long workday, we engaged in a conversation aimed at providing me with history as well as some insight into the current state of a new but growing movement.

Ana R., in her late thirties, came to Nicaragua from France in 1973. She was nineteen years old then, married to a Nicaraguan and with a one-month old daughter in her arms. Tall, with light hair, she is now a Nicaraguan citizen. Hazel, shorter and darker, is a young woman with a frank smile. She is from Matagalpa, the city to the north from where, I'm told, a good number of the "out" lesbians come. Much later she would remind me that she and my youngest daughter were in the same militia battalion when my daughter and I lived here in the early eighties. Carmen is from that part of northern Spain called Catalonia. She also came to work in Nicaragua out of her previous experience in the solidarity movement. Mary, another Matagalpa native, is a familiar face. I remember meeting her in the early days of the revolution. Ana V. is from Cost Rica. She works in the area of community health. Callie, also tall and blond, arrives late. She is from the United States. And finally, Amy is also a North American woman. Our paths have crossed on several occasions. She and Callie have each lived here for six years.

It's Hazel and Amy who begin by offering a brief picture of the origins of this movement, each remembering the details slightly differently. This is history in the process of being compiled. I want to know when lesbians and gay men first began to come together in more than a social context. What follows is a partial transcript of our conversation:

Hazel: We called it a collective. Or, that's the way we talk about it now. It started in 1985, that's when the first few women and men came together...

MR: What was the collective called? Did it have a name?

Hazel: No, at least not back then. It was a group of women and men who began getting together out of the need to talk to one another, in the atmosphere of prejudice that existed.

Amy: It was a difficult situation. Towards the end of 1985 a small group of lesbians and gay men began meeting. There were seven in all, six women and a man. They all lived in the same neighborhood, or were friends of people who lived there. At first it was just to talk about the issues they had: relationships, problems in the family, that sort of thing. For quite a while it was all very informal. Towards the end of 1986 they decided that they wanted to organize and began inviting friends. And a larger network emerged, because lots of people were still in the closet. People felt a terrible isolation...

MR: How did these people find one another?

Amy: When I got to Nicaragua at the end of '85 I found this group who knew one another, they lived in the same neighborhood. As a matter of fact, two women lived across the street from each other, right across the street and didn't even know it. People began coming together because one heard about another, rumors, that sort of thing, someone's reputation, old friendships.

In 1984 the Victoria Mercado Brigade came down from San Francisco. That's one of the first gay and lesbian brigades, that came to build a community center in Selim Shible.[10] Anyway, some of them looked up another North American woman who was working in that neighborhood, and she knew one of the women. From there on out, one got in touch with another. It was still *very* informal. Very underground.

MR: We're still talking about 1986?

Amy: Yes, towards the end of 1986. There'd already been a year of very informal gatherings. When there were fifty or so people showing up for meetings they elected a small coordinating committee, just to take minutes…

MR: Women and men…?

Amy: Women and men. A man and a woman were elected to co-coordinate the group. And they elected a treasurer to manage who knew what funds, because they never had any money; but in case they collected for something. And there was a woman who was an advisor. One of the early agreements was that you had to be politically involved. Most of these people were members of the FSLN, or of the Sandinista Youth Movement. Or they were active in the communities or at least sympathized with the revolution.

In December of that year, or January, 1987, a problem emerged. We were in a state of emergency[11] then, and everyone was on edge. Someone from State Security infiltrated the group, and we didn't figure it out until March, 1987. Suddenly people began receiving summons, to show up at the office of State Security. The first person called in was Rita, who was the advisor. Everyone kept quiet about all this, because it was a very dangerous time and no one wanted to make more problems for the FSLN than what they already had.

It was a mistake on the part of Security, but it was definitely an act of repression. Security really broke the group up. They said the only reason they weren't coming down harder was because they knew that those involved were Sandinistas. But they said that in a state of siege this kind of group couldn't exist, in fact that it could never exist.

MR: What reasons did they give? Was it an issue of "morality"…?

Amy: Yes. And they had their own morbid interest too. In the interviews they asked the women "how you do it." They asked a bunch of questions that really had nothing to do with politics.

MR: How long was Rita in prison?

Amy: Oh, just one day. For as long as the interrogation lasted. She wasn't tortured or anything, but they didn't treat her well. They didn't show her respect, they pressured her. And then they called all the rest of the group in and made them give declarations, sign papers, that sort of thing. It destroyed the group. And everyone took a vow of silence, because they felt that this could affect the international solidarity that was so badly needed. In many parts of the world solidarity with Nicaragua was headed by lesbians and gay men, and we knew that the reaction to what had happened could be terrible. It wasn't that we didn't want to act, but because of the political situation we felt that at the time speaking out could be worse for the movement we were building. We kept on working, silently, like an army of ants. The first time it was spoken about publicly was at the Gay and Lesbian Pride Celebration in June this year, and later in *La boletina*.[12]

Anyway, at the end of 1987 people doing AIDS work came to one of the public health conferences. The Public Health Ministry wanted to educate around safe sex, and they held some workshops for gay men. The government was interested in launching a campaign against AIDS, but when they invited a few men to participate the men insisted that the invitations be formal so they could show them to State Security, given that they had been warned never to try to organize or participate in gay activities again. Look, they said, this is a government invitation. Is it all right if we go? And of course they said it was.

They held workshops in the neighborhood clinics, at the Public Health Ministry, in different places. And the same five guys went to all of them. Because there weren't that many who were willing to go out to public clinics, in the community, and submit themselves to workers saying: There goes the faggot.... Not many wanted to make themselves vulnerable to that. That was when one of the most active of the men said: There's got to be another way.

So that's when Commander Dora María Téllez[13] called a meeting of all those who had been called in to State Security. She challenged them to do AIDS work within the lesbian and gay community. And they formed a popular education collective to fight AIDS, they distributed condoms, talked to people, mostly in the park in the center of Managua where a lot of men go to cruise. The group did some excellent work. The collective grew, it acquired its own history, and that's how the Nimehuatzín

Foundation got its start. We're talking about 1988...

MR: It's 1988 already?

Hazel: Well, the Foundation didn't really get off the ground until this year, 1991...

Amy: But its roots go back to 1988...

Hazel: There are so many versions, it would be interesting if we sat down one of these days and talked about all this, maybe even wrote it up...

MR: You're Nicaraguan. What part of the country are you from?

Hazel: I'm from Matagalpa. I came on the scene as a result of the AIDS education work that was being done. But by then the women decided that we wanted to meet on our own...

MR: Why was that?

Hazel: Because we felt that we had our own specific reality, as women. We wanted to analyze our condition as women. It was a period of consciousness raising. But we also continued our activities with the men. For example, on the tenth anniversary of the revolution we all turned out with our T-shirts, men and women together. It was our way of saying to the FSLN that after ten years of struggle we were there, we were Sandinistas and we were with the revolution. That was our first public appearance, so to speak.

MR: What kind of a reaction did that get?

Hazel: Well, we all formed a line, right when the National Directorate passed by [in the parade]. We wanted to make sure that they saw us so we all stood in a row, with our black T-shirts with the pink triangles. They just looked at us. Some laughed, some were serious, no one really said anything. But for us it was important. It was our collective coming out, you might say.

Our next big event was the party we held to commemorate the third anniversary of the day that State Security called members of the gay community in for interrogation. We invited the public, and the press. We showed a film called *Torch Song Trilogy* and invited people to ask questions, to express whatever concerns or questions they might have....

MR: That's a beautiful film...

Hazel: Yes. And we wanted to provoke a discussion. It was our first public observation of Gay Pride. That's when the press took notice, and they published interviews with some of us...

MR: What was the general attitude in the press?

Hazel: Mostly very positive. And where it wasn't all that positive it wasn't so much a negative attitude about lesbians and homosexuals as an atmosphere of questions, a reflection of the level of disinformation there is, I mean in society as a whole. And there were some very positive articles, where they interviewed women and men...

MR: What was the date of this event?

Hazel: June 30th, 1988. Gay Pride Day. It was a Sunday. Around that time some of us, women and men, also went to Mexico, to Acapulco, to participate in an international gathering of gays and lesbians. We went as a group, lesbians and gays together, not just the lesbians on our own. And that was something I noticed there, that outside of Nicaragua there's a lot of separation, lesbians working with lesbians and gay men working with other gay men, a lot of division between the two.

Also, it seemed to us that internationally the European model was more in evidence. So the Latin Americans there felt the need to become acquainted with our reality, do our own networking so we could get to know what was going on in the different countries and get to know each other, exchange information and become closer. So we held an assembly and decided to form a network of our own. We named a provisional committee made up of twelve people, six delegates and six alternates, all from the countries of the Americas. We wanted to convoke a meeting of our own.

MR: What countries are represented among the delegates?

Hazel: Mexico, Peru, Puerto Rico, Nicaragua, Argentina, and the United States—that is, the Chicanos who live in the United States. Those are the delegates. The alternates are from Costa Rica, the Dominican Republic, Mexico, Argentina, and Brazil. Nicaragua holds the delegate seat for Central America, with the alternate being from Costa Rica. For now, what we're doing is sending out a questionnaire so we can find out who's out there, what the different groups are called. We want to invite them all to a meeting in 1993. That's where we're hoping to give birth to the future Latin American and Caribbean network.

We're just beginning to understand our realities. For example, in Acapulco some people had a very negative attitude towards the Latinos who live in the United States. They in turn often felt excluded, like the rest of us didn't consider them Latin Americans anymore, and they are struggling to become accepted as Latins who have lived for years in the United States, dealing with people who say they have all these advantages we don't have, more freedom and all that. We want to break with these prejudices, with the different walls that exist.

MR: I wanted to ask you something about your own history, Hazel. How is it that, growing up in a small town like Matagalpa, you came out of the closet?

Hazel: Well, it was a process. I considered myself heterosexual at first. I didn't know I was a lesbian. I began to understand that I was around 1981 but I didn't come out right away. I didn't even assume it fully. Around then I started living as a bisexual. And even that brought me problems, because I was a member of the FSLN and bisexuality was seen as political deviation. They said that bisexuals and homosexuals could easily be bought by the enemy, utilized in ways that could hurt the revolution. It became an ideological conflict for me.

But my history is an interesting one, because I made a trip to Cuba about then. And you might say that's where I really began to accept myself as a lesbian. It's contradictory, because Cuba is a country where homosexuality has been heavily persecuted. Still, I grew a lot there. I began going around with other lesbians and gay men. Before that, in Nicaragua, even though I had a relationship with a woman I never really had a community. In Cuba I found a *massive* community. An enormous parallel world. I'd never seen so many lesbians and gay men in my life. You could go to *un lugar de ambiente*[14] and most people wouldn't have known that's what it was. Except that everyone there was gay. So when I returned to Nicaragua from that first trip to Cuba, I began to identify as a lesbian. And then I returned to Cuba.

I went to study at the film school, and of course, in the world of artists, well it's even more accepted. I met students from all over Latin America, from Africa and Asia, and I got to know much more about lesbian and gay culture, what was happening on other continents, I met a lot more people. That's when I really came out. I learned to live my lesbianism much more completely. At the school there were no prejudices at all, we had complete freedom to do whatever we wanted, live together, whatever. So when I came back to Nicaragua in 1988 I began to meet with the lesbian group I mentioned before. From then on, it's all been much easier.

[Carmen has been listening. Now it looks like she has something to say.]

Carmen: I come from the feminist movement in Spain. Actually, I came to Nicaragua as a heterosexual. It's here that I had my first relationship with a woman. I began working with the different women's groups.

When I fell in love with a Nicaraguan woman, that's when I decided to support the work being done by the lesbians. The group was already functioning, and in spite of the fact that I didn't have any prior experience, I thought: This is where I can put my efforts.

MR: When did you come to Nicaragua?

Carmen: In April, 1989. So I was in on the beginnings of the group that started at the end of that year. And that became my main area of work. Although the group had its good and bad moments. But I was a part of that. I was a feminist and had always supported a person's right to their sexual preference, and obviously, from the moment I came out as a lesbian, that became more important to me. I'm a doctor and I also work in sex education. So I've been concerned about the degree of homophobia there is, in the population as a whole and even among some of the leadership cadre.

I don't know if you heard about the letter that was published a week ago. There's been a tendency here to call feminists lesbians, as a way of making them look bad, tarnishing their reputations. Our argument has been to insist that there are lesbians everywhere, market women, professionals, Sandinistas. That we're as responsible as anyone else, as serious, as hard-working. But we need to do a lot more work around this.

Ana V.: I'm from Costa Rica. But then, that's right next door. And, well, my history is a bit different. I came to Nicaragua as a lesbian, with my partner who was already living here. But I didn't join the group until about six months ago, maybe a year. I've always functioned in heterosexual society. Everyone where I worked knew I was a lesbian. I never felt any particular prejudice. My co-workers were men, they all knew it, and they accepted me fine.

MR: This was in Nicaragua?

Ana V.: Yes, in Nicaragua.

MR: Because I know there is a movement in Costa Rica as well. I've met Costa Rican lesbians who tell me they have gay bars in San José…

Ana V.: It's a different kind of movement there. Not as linked to politics, or to the idea of changing society. In Nicaragua it's very much a part of all that. In Costa Rica you have the homosexual's struggle within the context of a struggle for human rights. Here it's much broader. It's the struggle to make society as a whole more comprehensive, more open. For that reason it's much more interesting. In Costa Rica you end up in a ghetto, something that hasn't happened here, at least not yet. Here we've wanted to push society so it will make a place for us, not carve out a place which is only for lesbians and gay men. I think this makes for a stronger fight against homophobia in general.

Carmen: I'm interested in how we can do this work, fight against society's homophobia. Because it seems to me that the worst homophobia of all is inside the revolutionary movement itself. AMNLAE's attitude really affected me. It hurt me deeply. I wasn't that surprised, but it hurts to hear women labeling other women "lesbian" as a way of denigrating them. And I know that as a foreigner it's not my job to lead this struggle. It's up to the Nicaraguan sisters to do that. But we need to intensify this work, in all the different sectors. Among the youth. In our sex education. Because the prejudices run very deep.

When I think about how the sisters and brothers who were repressed back in '87 were reduced to silence. Or they chose to be silent because they supported the revolution. Some were members of the FSLN, their organization said that being gay was a deviancy and they were afraid of being kicked out unless they stayed in the closet. That silence is a terrible thing. I think about how hard it's been. It's taken four years for that silence to be broken. And now AMNLAE comes out with that article…

MR: Four years of silence can be hard, a day of silence can be hard. On the other hand, four years isn't much when you think about homophobia and heterosexism everywhere, how deeply rooted in society these prejudices are. I think what Ana said about the difference between a place like Nicaragua and other countries is interesting. In spite of the official repression at one point, it seems to me there is more openness now. Maybe particularly now, since the elections, when the FSLN is no longer the party in power and all sorts of issues have surfaced…

Ana V.: There are basic differences, especially in the ways that certain values are being changed, which permit this type of space, this type of discussion, these concerns. Because in capitalism the whole legal aspect, even the definition of morality, is more developed. The value structure is more defined, everything in neat little packages. In this sense, the Sandinista revolution opened up a space that maybe didn't transform things completely but it certainly didn't close off the possibility.

In spite of the official repression you had here at a particular moment in time, most people, I mean the general population, have a lot of questions about sexuality. And this makes it easier to talk about taboos. Among the youth, especially, we have the opportunity of talking about all sorts of things, including different sexual options.

MR: In the United States the word "lesbian" continues to be an epithet, used by many conservatives, fundamentalist Christians and the like, against feminists, or against women who are political, whether or not they are gay. I was involved in an immigration case, for example, for five years, and I wasn't yet out as a lesbian. But frequently in the press or on the radio when someone wanted to insult me they'd call me a lesbian. It seems to me that what's happening here is extraordinarily positive, in spite of the obstacles.

Hazel: One of the most successful things is the work being done by homosexuals in the struggle against AIDS. They work a lot among gay men who, you might say, live on the edge. Because in the poorer neighborhoods there are men who sell themselves in order to survive. And the brigades teach them safe sex, give them condoms.

Another thing we're trying to do now is to open up a place where people can come, not just for political work, but *un lugar de ambiente*, a place where lesbians and gay men can get together socially. Although, you know, I heard something today that's got me worried. It seems that some of the entrepreneurial folk who have come back from Miami are opening a club over in El Carmen. That worries me. In the first place because they're going to make a lot of money. But also because it's going to be run by those folks that have come back from Miami, with their money mentality. I can just imagine what kind of a place it's going to be. And then people who support the FSLN will have to open our own place in reaction to that. And it won't be like the work we've been trying to do, creating a certain kind of consciousness, making it possible for us to understand ourselves, our own reality first, and then getting together more publicly. It's been a long and hard process and I don't like it that all of a sudden, because UNO thinks of opening up a place like this, there are two places, disconnected with what we've been doing.

Mary: I wanted to say something else. Inside the FSLN it hasn't just been repression towards homosexuals. I'm a product of my own particular history of course, but my experience hasn't been anything like what you've been talking about here. I'm a long-time member of the FSLN. My comrades have always known I'm a lesbian. No one's ever accused me of anything, and no one's ever refused me positions of responsibility because of my sexuality. I've always had positions of responsibility.

In a Sandinista Assembly they've even said officially that no reprisals would be taken against anyone because of his or her sexual preference. I'm not saying that this policy has always been carried out, that there haven't been people who have done what they wanted. But it's depended a lot on who happens to be in charge, on what kind of a human being that person is, their amplitude, their vision.

I'm not speaking only for myself. I know a lot of Sandinistas who are gay, and who have never been expelled from the party because of that. Of course it's been hard. We've had to fight to show that we are as good as anyone else, like any group about which prejudice exists. I'm not denying that. But it's also true that there are many of us who are known to be gay and have been accepted.

This is something that's made an impression on people from other places. For example, a Colombian comrade and I were talking once and she told me how surprised she was that the Sandinista Front had known homosexuals in its ranks. She said that couldn't happen in Colombia. That comrade was also surprised that homosexuals were revolutionaries, not rightists. And I think that most of us here in Nicaragua are progressive, or we try to be revolutionaries, or we *are* revolutionaries.

And I think this is something that the movement here in Nicaragua has given to the rest of Latin America; it's made others stop and think about the fact that homosexuals can be revolutionaries. It's a small contribution we've made. I think what Ana said about not creating ghettos is important. We need to defend our place in society as a whole, make society respect us for what we are, for what we do, for our work.

MR: I'm really interested in what you're saying about demanding social space. In the United States, at least in certain areas and in certain professions or trades, in our political life or as writers or artists, we have come to the point where many of us can be out. We've struggled for that space, and to some extent we've won it. In my own case, I demand that my partner be recognized as such, at least as far as that's possible.

On the other hand, at least at this point in time, I don't think I'd feel comfortable going dancing with her at a mixed club. There's too much homophobia. It's too dangerous out there. We feel more comfortable, at least for now, going dancing where we know we're accepted. And that's among other lesbians, and sometimes gay men.

Hazel: Here there's some discussion around that. But I want to say that I disagree with Mary. Because the FSLN, as a party, *did* repress the group of gays and lesbians. It respected those who were gay but didn't make waves. If you stayed in the closet, that was fine. But when you started a group, a movement, it was something else. Although I agree that the revolution opened up the space that made it possible for us to wage this struggle. And our struggle has helped other gays feel socially accepted.

Ana V.: There are exceptions. There's a group of gay men in El Viejo, there must be 80 or 90 of them. And that's a peasant population, in banana country. These guys are all ages and they're accepted in their community. They have parties in the streets, street fairs, they participate in all sorts of events, and it hasn't been easy.

Hazel: There's also a difference between men and women. It's not the same for lesbians and gay men because there's always the matter of *machismo*. It's always easier for the men. Men exercise their male privilege even when they dance together. But if you're a woman dancing with another woman, right away some guy is going to come up and say: "What's this? Imagine!" And he'll ask you to dance because he can't even conceive of the fact that you'd prefer a woman over him!

Several voices: …Yeah…butting in and…

MR: I look at the last few years of Sandinista struggle, before the elections, and I think about how hard it must have been. All

143

sorts of issues were sacrificed, abortion for instance. And in retrospect I think many of us agree that those sacrifices were mistakes. But at the time I wonder how much was due to homophobia and how much was simply the fear of going out on a limb at a time when defending the process itself demanded so much energy. I'm not excusing homophobia. I'm just wondering if we can expect so much in such difficult periods...

Hazel: There are plenty of homophobes in the FSLN, I can tell you...

MR: Everywhere...

Hazel: Sure, there are homophobes everywhere. But look, it's not that I expected the FSLN to make some kind of a pronouncement. It would have been enough if they'd have let us be. Because if you're going to let some be because they're in the closet, but come down on others because they're not, that's not right.

Mary: I'm not denying that there's been repression, at least against the group that started organizing. The thing you have to understand is that many of us weren't ourselves anymore. We stopped being ourselves in support of a cause. There were lots of things we pushed aside because we believed in that cause. In many cases we forgot about our personal life, about attending to our own personal issues.

When we lost the election, that's when I began to pay attention to my personal life, that's when I began to *have* a personal life. And this isn't just my story; it's a phenomenon shared by many of us. I'd say that a great many Nicaraguans are experiencing this, maybe the whole 40% that voted for the FSLN. I think we need a more profound analysis of all this now...

Carmen: I think that all this has to do with the issue of feminism, too. Feminism is something that was always relegated to a secondary place here. I mean there was an official women's organization and all that, but the real feminist issues weren't addressed. Issues like abortion, sexuality, family planning. It doesn't do much good to stay in the past. We have to learn from our mistakes. Revolutionary struggle always has its contradictions. It couldn't be otherwise, because we are human beings and humans have our contradictions. We need to deal with the contradictions, but simultaneously, not try to pretend that some things must be done first and the rest can wait.

I belong to a revolutionary organization too, and I think that the struggle around women's rights is just as important as the struggle for the economy, as the struggle for workers' rights, respect for sexual preference. Like Mary says, we have to learn from our history. We understand there was a time when all that mattered was survival, we lived through that. But that's changed now. And I think we have to promote an educational process among militants...when I say militants I mean members of the Party.

Mary: I agree. But I ask myself, right now, how do we do this? If you think about it, there's a huge vacuum right now, and no one has yet found a way of dealing with that. Political life in this country is in pretty bad shape. We're lying if we say that any of us have a structured political life at this point. Each of us has gotten behind some social flag or other: women's rights, community work, work with the farmers, whatever. But Party life as such just doesn't exist here now.

MR: What I've felt in the short time I've been back is that an understanding of feminism, not an understanding of the need for a gay and lesbian movement but even an understanding of feminism itself, is not very prevalent among the FSLN leadership. I'm talking about feminism as an important ideology, a conception of power, a way of looking at the world, feminism in the broadest sense. It seems to me that there aren't very many among the highest level of leadership—maybe two or three at the most—who even understand what feminism means. I was surprised...

Callie: I know that in different parts of the country there are women who are working hard, doing important work individually or in mixed groups. But sometimes I think that the struggle for women's rights—and I'm not talking about women having power, I'm talking about them simply having rights, the most elemental rights to their own reproduction, whatever—that's a struggle that's very incipient in the countryside.

MR: What kind of work do you do?

Callie: I work with public health promoters and I travel around...in the mountains, beyond Jinotega.

MR: How long have you been doing that?

Callie: I've been with my current project for the past three years. But I've been working in the countryside here since 1985. Of course the Sixth Region[15] is one of the most backward. Maybe in the Fourth Region things are better...

Ana V.: I think you're right. I work in Region One with a project for peasant women at the state level, where we begin with such primary discussions as children's sexuality. It's a project that deals with women's health. I couldn't agree more. The thing is, if we're going to talk about feminism in Nicaragua at least for the moment we're basically going to be talking about Managua. We're going to be talking about one small group of Association of Farm Workers women who've been privy to an educational process that's by no means generalized.

But Mary said something I want to pick up on, which is that right now there really isn't such a thing as the FSLN. What there is, is a lot of different people in a lot of different political movements and, well, we're still out there. That's important. And it's the result of a revolutionary process that's also been very important. The fact that a year after the kind of electoral defeat we've had you've got a whole society involved in this kind of dynamic, concrete struggles, this says you've got a process that's still very much alive.

And on top of your own personal problem of how to put food on the table—because we've got to remember that in Nicaragua right now most people are simply trying to survive—but beyond the struggle for survival, there's a movement of women talking about our rights. And that's more than you have in many other places.

MR: I can see that the revolution is very much alive. It's alive in the concrete struggles that continue and it's also alive in people's consciousness. A consciousness has been created here that in many other Latin American countries has yet to be created…only in countries where political organization has been high, like Uruguay, Bolivia, countries like those. In the United States we don't have anything like the kind of generalized consciousness you have here. And this, for me, is a tangible product of ten years of revolution.

Hazel: There's something I want to say, and it's about peasant women, women in the countryside in Nicaragua. They might not know what the word feminism means, they might not use that word. But in their lives, in their everyday practice, in the way they express the need for change, they understand very well what feminism is. For example, I was involved in a study about women's mortality in childbirth. It was in the context of trying to legalize abortion. And what I found was that peasant women understood very well their need to stop having so many children. They don't want those huge families anymore. They may not know how to avoid them, what to use, but at the feeling level they're clear. If you mention the word *abortion*, for example, you'll hear "Ay, no, no, no, by the Holy Virgin no!" But they'll try to abort all the same. The thing is, they'll go out on their own and try to solve the problem, because their objective conditions force them to. Or about their men: they won't talk about sexism, they won't use that word, but they'll talk about how their men make them pregnant and then move on to a younger woman across the way, leaving them to deal with the children, life, everything. Peasant women are tired of being treated like that, they don't want to go on that way.

And something else. This is something I was told, because I also worked with a group of midwives. They told me one of them got called to attend to a woman, and it turned out that the woman's husband showed up. He was drunk. He started beating up on his wife and she lost the baby. This happens a lot. And all those women together lynched that man. They all fell on him at once. So what I'm saying is that everyday life in the countryside teaches women about sexism and they respond. They may not articulate it with the same words we use. But they're tired of it. They don't want to go on like they are.

The other day I was somewhere where they'd given out something like 1,000 *manzanas*.[16] It turned into an all-male cooperative. Something like six men ended up with most of the land. They only wanted to give three *manzanas* to the women. Well, the women planted some bushes. And in one of their meetings the men began to attack them for being stupid, what did they want to be planting bushes for, who knows what all. But those bushes proved nourishing to the cows, you know? So when the men began having trouble finding feed, they told the women: Give us what you planted and we'll give you three *manzanas* of land.

The women said: No. Each of these bushes is worth five pesos. And the men tried to threaten them. But the women stood their ground. There are a lot more women than men, because there are a lot of women without husbands. The six men began calling them names, whores, crazy women, whatever. But the women are standing their ground. They're coming together, they're organizing, and they're dealing with the situation. So I think...

Callie: I think there's something else we have to understand. I don't know about other parts of the country, but in the Sixth Region we've got the influence of the church, the Catholic Church and the evangelical churches. I've seen things change.

Before, women were more open about a lot of things, sex education, family planning, maybe not so much about abortion. But now it feels like we're going backwards. The church is everywhere, and I can see the change. The women go to mass, the kids go to their catechism classes, and I could see the difference in a sex education workshop we did. They start talking about religion. What the priests tell them and what we say produces a conflict in the women. Especially in the most remote areas... .

It's getting late. We all acknowledge exhaustion as we say good night. I know that these women will rise early tomorrow to begin another day on whatever job faces them. Some will still return to offices or go on to other meetings tonight. It's been a productive exchange, one in an ongoing series of such exchanges among women who are struggling to change our own reality and the world.

—Fall, 1991

Notes

1. First published in an earlier version, in *Signs, Journal of Women in Culture and Society: Theorizing Lesbian Experience* ,Chicago: The University of Chicago Press, Summer 1993, pp. 907-924.

2. *Inside the Nicaraguan Revolution: The Story of Doris Maria Tijerino*, Vancouver, New Star Books, 1978; *Sandino's Daughters*, Vancouver, New Star Books, 1981; *Christians in the Nicaraguan Revolution*, Vancouver, New Star Books, 1983; *Risking a Somersault in the Air: Conversations with Nicaraguan Writers*, San Francisco, Solidarity Publications, 1984; *Gathering Rage: The Failure of Twentieth Century Revolutions to Develop a Feminist Agenda*, New York City, Monthly Review of Books, 1993; and *Sandino's Daughters Revisited*, New Brunswick, New Jersey, Rutgers University Press, 1994 and (for Canadian consumption) Vancouver, New Star Books, 1994.

3. *Frente Sandinista de Liberación Nacional* (Sandinista National Liberation Front), the political and military organization that coordinated the Nicaraguan people's successful overthrow of the dictatorship of Anastasio Somoza in 1979. The FSLN was founded in 1961 by a handful of revolutionaries, who took their courage, some strategies, and their name from the earlier history of Augusto C. Sandino, the peasant leader who fought Somoza's father and the U.S. Marines in the 1920s and '30s.

4. Based on the early design Magaly Pineda contributed to when she worked for the Nicaraguan Ministry of Public Welfare during the first months of the Sandinista revolution.

5. The FSLN held its First Congress after its electoral defeat, in July of 1991. At that time there was a strong movement to include at least one woman on the Directorate; Dora María Téllez was the obvious candidate. But once again the old boy's club prevailed, and Téllez was not permitted to fill one of the two vacancies. In May, 1994, the FSLN held what they called an extraordinary congress. There the National Directorate was expanded from nine to 15 seats, and five women were included (as well as several men stepping down and others added). The new women members are Mónica Baltodano, Mirna Cunningham, Benigna Mendiola, Dora María Téllez, and Dorotea Wilson.

6. The women interviewed in these pages provide an overview of gay rights during and since the decade of Sandinista government. Since this was written, in June, 1992, the governing UNO coalition introduced Article #205 of the Penal Code, a tough anti-sodomy law. Although all Sandinista delegates and two conservatives voted against the article, the National Assembly passed it by a narrow margin. And President Violeta Barrios de Chamorro failed to exercise her veto. To date the law has not been utilized, and there is a many-pronged and growing movement against it. More recently, Nicaragua's Supreme Court upheld the statute.

7. *Asociación de mujeres nicaragüenses Luisa Amanda Espinosa* (The Luisa Amanda Espinosa Association of Nicaraguan Women), a mass women's organization which had its roots in the years of struggle and evolved in different ways during the ten years of popular government. Luisa Amanda Espinosa was a working-class woman believed to have been the first female member of the FSLN to fall in battle. She was killed in April of 1970.

8. *Revueltos* translates as scrambled or mixed up; many of those who took up arms with the U.S.-sponsored counterrevolutionary forces and those who came out of the Sandinista tradition have joined together demanding land, work, survival. In the northern city of Ocotal, such a group *of women only* call themselves the *Frente Nora Astorga* (Nora Astorga Front). In memory of a Sandinista heroine who died in 1989, they have organized and

armed themselves. Their demands include work, reforestation, day care, women's clinics, and sewing machines.

9. I was in Managua to attend a meeting of the international solidarity movement, called by the Sandinist National Liberation Front (FSLN) to discuss the results of its recent Congress and share prospects for further work. Particularly interested in what women are thinking and how they feel in the context of the changes that have taken place in their country, I met with as many as was feasible during the week I was there. This transcript comes mainly from one of several conversations and is also informed by others.

10. A Managua neighborhood, named after one of the early Sandinista martyrs, victim of the Somoza era.

11. Because of the Contra war, the government decreed what was to be an ongoing state of siege.

12. *La boletina: un aporte a la comunicación entre mujeres* (The Bulletin: A Contribution to Women's Communication) is a small but vital publication, the first issue of which appeared in July, 1991. It includes news and analysis about Nicaraguan women. Subscriptions are welcome and can be obtained by sending U.S. $25.00 for one year to Puntos de Encuentro, Apartado Postal RP-39, Managua, Nicaragua.

13. High-level Sandinista leader, Minister of Public Health at the time.

14. A gay bar or gathering place.

15. During the Sandinista government, the country was divided into regions.

16. A *manzana* is a measurement of land.

Santiago General Cemetery

Victor Jara's grave

Santiago General Cemetery, in front of Victor Jara's grave

"Patio 29," Santiago General Cemetery

5

Gracias a la Vida[1]

—for Ana and Louis

✳

Gracias a la vida que me ha dado tanto…

I give thanks to life for it has given me so much, sang Violeta Para, the great Chilean folksinger who wove her spell from a circus tent in one of Santiago's parks. That was the first *peña*, a place where poets and musicians and young people came to turn their pain and vision into song. Latin America's New Song Movement emerged from that tent and set up residence worldwide.

Violeta didn't live to see a people's government voted into power in 1970. She put a gun to her head three years earlier— legend says it was the unreturned love of a younger man. But when Popular Unity arrived—the first democratically elected socialist government in the Americas—her spirit must have danced. Three years the experiment lasted, three years of people reclaiming their copper and their energies.

Three years, too, in which the United States prepared and supported an elaborate take-back. On September 11, 1973 Chilean General Augusto Pinochet and the U.S. Central Intelligence Agency pulled off a military coup that left a wake of torture, disappearance, and death, so overwhelming that it has had to be excised from official memory as the years unfold.

Although these events are barely two decades old there are many who do not remember. As in our country young people think of Vietnam as a movie location, do not recognize names like Trujillo, Batista, or Somoza, and believe that people would have jobs if only they weren't so lazy, memory has been bent to fit the victors' version of history. Neo-liberalism is the new Latin

American flag. Its stained cloth wipes the crevices of recall until a woman running a boarding house can smile and say: "But it was a civil war we had here; if some were killed, that's just the way it is." And then, as if to make her point completely: "And anyway, they probably deserved it."

In the center of a street map of Santiago de Chile the General Cemetery is a sprawling unevenly shaped expanse of green. The Catholic Cemetery, separated by a street or two, is slightly smaller and much more exclusive, "where the truly rich are buried," Gladys tells me later.

My friend Gladys has returned, one of thousands of exiles, under the umbrella of this new "democracy." This painful face-lift that has remade the downtown capital, and makes walking its upscaled streets seem like walking in Boston or San Francisco—except that *some* of the signs are in Spanish.

Many who did not escape, those with names and those still nameless, are joined in the General Cemetery's unquiet expanse. As we enter through the broad gate off Recoletta Avenue I am met by the hot wind of their voices, hoarse sound bytes of memory. Three of us make this pilgrimage: my daughter Ana, who has come to study in this place; her partner Louis who is with her here; and me, a visitor.

I was last in Chile in the fall of 1972. The Popular Unity government was threatened but still vibrant then. Great murals brightened public walls. You could feel the energy of people working for possibility. The truck owners' strike was in full force and a strict 11 p.m. curfew meant I'd sleep each night wherever the hour found me.

Twenty years. No easy way to describe or decipher the process by which a people can be broken, but silencing memory is certainly a big part of it. The city is modernized almost beyond recognition. The *poblaciones*, those old fighting shanty towns that once rimmed the urban area, have disappeared. Pinochet murdered many of their inhabitants, then built "model" housing for those who were left, disheveled high-rises with water and electricity but no soul.

I think of Roque Dalton's poem about another dictator in yet another Latin American country:

> They say he was a good President
>   because he built cheap housing
>   for the Salvadorans who survived...[2]

La Moneda, the palace where a Comrade President was forced to take his own life, looks as it did before the bombs and cannon blasts drew flames and funnels of black smoke from its classic facade. Two large black dogs now run and jump across a perfect lawn. One soldier in Prussian dress stands guard before the main door.

Throughout the city, soldiers are everywhere: protecting banks and other public buildings: the *milicos* with their instruments of war. The *carabineros* or police are more mobile, arriving in a rush of vehicles: small black and white vans with their insignia of crossed rifles like the crossed bones of old pirate flags.

People walk quietly. Numbed. They speak quietly in that soft lilting Spanish that almost always rises gently at the end of a sentence. "*Claro...*" meaning both "of course" and "do you understand?" A manifest courtesy, though not as simple as it often sounds. Scarred fields of memory rise and fall behind the eyes. We enter a neighborhood shop to buy a piece of bread. Customers stand patiently in several lines.

Having chosen the loaf we want, we must join a line to receive a small white swatch of paper. *Esos papelitos*, we say, laughing. Another line eventually ends before the person who will verify that what has been entered on this paper is correct—then add another, stapling the two together. After a third line the stapled slips are examined by someone whose single task it is to do so. We pay. And a fourth employee hands us our bread. It is the way things are done. And none of the several workers would consider doing another's job.

Still, there are cracks in the facade. The waiter who follows Ana and Louis out of the restaurant and tells them his father voted for Allende. The beauty-parlor attendant who catches Ana's eye for one transparent second as a customer praises the General and says she dreams nightly of Pinochet: her personal Savior. Later the attendant tells Ana she cannot speak here, but wants her to know she does not agree. "We must meet and talk," she insists, "I will tell you about the disappeared in my own family…"

Entering the General Cemetery is like slipping through one of these instantaneous cracks. I reach around myself and remember to keep on breathing. "We'd like to visit Víctor Jara's grave," Ana says to an elderly man in dark blue overalls. Gardener or gravedigger, perhaps both. "Can you tell us where it is?"

"You'll never find it," he asserts. "Here, this gentleman will go with you…" And a second blue-overalled worker climbs quickly into the car. Waving us past the pay point, he signals to the guard "It's okay. They're with me."

Brief fragments of conversation cut this overcast morning as we travel along narrow grave-lined streets: "Go on…keep going…turn right here…take a left…" Where the old families are buried, mausoleums rise in varying manifestations of wealth. The names are recognizable, even to a visitor: Montt, O'Higgins, Pratt, Allende….

As class status diminishes, collective walls replace the single monuments. In these the dead are buried in tiers, five or six stories high. Here and there little balconies support vases of flowers ,or planters hold more permanent gardens. Canvas awnings, tiny grill-work gates, miniature columns, statuettes, religious icons, personal notes: messages from the living to the dead—or from the living to the living.

It is before one of these shelved walls that we finally stop on the far side of this crowded terrain. Our guide points to Jara's tomb, four levels up. Behind a low stone wall fresh flowers almost obscure the singer's name, cut awkwardly and painted in black upon the plain cement. Below the name is "September 1973," the date that marks too many of this cemetery's resting places. Above the name and to the right in much smaller letters are the inscriptions "Gigi 91" and "Leno 91." We do not know what they mean.

"Thank you, *Don*," Ana says, using the formal Sir. And then, "What is your name?"

He seems taken aback. "My name doesn't matter..."

"I just wanted to be able to address you by it," Ana insists, by way of explanation.

But the man remains silent.

"Would you like me to take some of the flowers away, just for a moment, so you can read the inscription?" He has seen that I am trying to record this place with my camera.

"Yes," I smile gratefully. And he hops up onto the wall to clear the obscuring display.

Two young trees in front of Jara's tomb bear recent messages to the Communist songwriter and singer. One message records lines from a song: *"Mi canto es de los andamios / para alcanzar las estrellas....* My song is scaffolding / to reach the stars." On a photograph of Jara with an inward gaze and about to extract a cigarette from between his lips are the dates 20.IX.32 and 16.IX.73. September, month of death and renovation.

Víctor Jara was rounded up with thousands in the days following the coup. In the Chile Stadium—one of several detention centers—the story goes, they made him play his guitar and sing, while they tortured and murdered those around him and finally shattered his wrists.

Then they shot him.

And he kept on singing.

Later the words of his last song surfaced, smuggled out of the stadium. They sound today, an echoing bridge to the brutality of those days and months, and years:

> There are five thousand of us here
> in this small part of the city...
> here alone are ten thousand hands
> that plant seeds

and make the factories run…
Let…the world
cry out against this atrocity!
We are ten thousand hands
that can produce nothing…
How hard it is to sing
when I must sing of horror…[3]

We turn from the wall. And unexpectedly find ourselves facing long rows of black metal crosses, hundreds or thousands, most bearing the simple *N. N.—ningún nombre*, no name—of the "disappeared." This is *Patio 29* of a cemetery permanently defaced by fascism. This is where the army brought many of the bodies.

The section was only revealed to the public a few years back, following the plebiscite in which a startling majority of Chilean voters refused to say yes to Pinochet as president for life. It was then that forensic specialists were able to trace some of the bodies' identities, adding names where there had only been questions, waiting.

As we stand there drained of feeling, trying to absorb the weight of these rows of simple crosses, our unnamed guide begins to speak. Disconnected phrases lurch from his lips. He says he has been working in this cemetery for 31 years, digging graves, sweeping the walkways, cleaning weeds, attending to the dead. He is trying to tell us what it was like in September of 1973 when they began bringing the caskets in. Dozens. Then hundreds.

"We stayed late each night," he says. "We worked all night long. Night after night. And all day too. *Estos son los hijos del Pinoccio*—these are Pinochio's children."[4] With sad irony.

The man's words come in a flat tone, bursts of broken sound. He knows we cannot understand but feels the need to witness. We know we cannot understand but need this piece to place among the others in the puzzle heavy in our hands. We stand staring at *Patio 29's* long even rows until I hear my own voice reaching back from some distant place:

"Would you take us to Allende's grave?"

Our guide nods. We get back in the car and retrace our route, past a slow funeral—mourners following the casket on foot—to the better-tended areas where members of the wealthier families rest. Among ornate chapels, their iron gates locked fast against intrusion, the Comrade President's two white marble spires rise. An etched plaque beneath a scattering of wilted carnations bears Allende's final words: "One day, the great avenues will open and the people will walk through…" The fading tap of that static-burdened radio emission repeats itself inside my skull.

Down a curve of steps is the crypt itself. Only two of the Allende-Bussi burial shelves are occupied as yet: one with Salvador, the other with his daughter Beatríz. I remember her suicide in Cuba, 1977. She was a doctor, had been her father's closest collaborator, was in the palace with him that morning of September 11th, her belly big with the child she would soon give birth to. He ordered her out, along with the others, "to tell the world what happened here." And she did leave and did tell of it, but finally wasn't able to make her peace with the separation.

So now they lie together, behind the white marble. "His daughter," our guide reiterates, "as a woman, you should be interested in her."

I don't even find the comment strange.

I continue to shoot my camera. He continues to suggest images I might want. And then: "You know, photography is not allowed in this cemetery."

I gesture incredulity—then complicity.

"It's okay," he assures me, "you came at the right time. The guards are on their morning coffee break…"

And then, his voice swelling with thousands of voices:

"We were waiting for your visit."

—Spring in Santiago / late fall in Albuquerque, 1993

Notes

1. First published in *IKON* #14/15, New York City, Spring 1994.
2. "General Martínez" by Roque Dalton, *Taberna y otros lugares*, Casa de las Américas, Havana, Cuba, 1969. Translation by M.R.
3. Fragment of Víctor Jara's last song, written and smuggled out of the Chile Stadium, September 1973. From *An Unfinished Song: The Life of Víctor Jara* by Joan Jara, Ticknor & Fields, New York, 1984.
4. In guarded voices or in the privacy of their homes, those who despise Pinochet call him Pinocchio, the liar. It is a play on his name and on the internationally popular children's tale.

Street scene, Havana

Family practice doctor dispensing free vitamins in
Havana neighborhood

Street scene, Santa Clara

Beach, Santa María del Mar

May 1st, 1993, Havana

May 1st, 1993, Havana

Fifi, head of construction project, Havana

Havana

Cigar factory, Santa Clara

Cigar factory, Santa Clara

Cigar factory, Santa Clara

Che Guevara Day Care Center, Santa Clara

Cathedral, Havana

Street scene, Havana

6

Return to Cuba
Some Stories

❊

The air is warm and moist. Sun shines on the familiar billboards urging more production, less waste, unity. Clusters of school children in their familiar uniforms: the color of skirt or pants indicating teacher's training, vocational, regular elementary, or higher education. People waiting at bus stops, decently dressed and healthy. None of the homeless—so familiar where we live—pleading for work or food. None of the hungry kids who swarm the cities of other Latin American countries.

These observations as we drive from Rancho Boyeros into Havana provide my first challenge to recent news reports and eye-witness accounts attesting to the Cuban revolution's imminent demise. I remind myself it's been predicted for years. Our bus shares the road with ancient trucks and hundreds of bicycles as we make our way through a semi-industrial area. Then, just past the Sports Palace's round dome, Revolutionary Square opens before us. José Martí, his marble figure gazing over the scene of so many historic gatherings, seems to be telling me:

"Relax. It's hard times, but it's not over 'til it's over."

Across the aisle on the charter from Miami a woman is crying. Her tears move silently down intensely rouged cheeks. One falls on a medley of gold bracelets at her wrist. She discreetly pats it away with the satin of her other sleeve. Face and body are immobile: no sound or tremor betray this woman's feelings, but the intensity of her emotion pulls me from my own powerful memories as we almost brush the tops of palms and the plane's captain announces that in minutes we'll be landing at Havana's José

Martí International Airport.

Is she a Cuban living on the island who has visited family on the other side and is coming apart on her return? Or is she an exiled Cuban approaching her homeland for the first time in many years? I can only guess at this woman's age, hidden on the surfaces of a face sculpted by beauticians and clothiers and will. Dark mascara slips now, churning with rouge and the ache of goodbye or of hello. Our plane lands. We scatter. I do not see the woman again.

I lived in Cuba from 1969 through 1980. I raised my children there (two of the four were graduated from the University of Havana), worked as an editor, translator, and journalist, wrote a dozen books—among them two oral histories of Cuban women—and learned photography by apprenticing to a local photographic genius. Back in 1978 I began to frame my images without film in the camera; it was scarce and there was a lot to grasp before wasting what we had. I loved and wrote poems and cried in this city. Its landscape of palms and weathered colonial buildings was bedrock to eleven years of my life.

A dozen years later the world is a different place. The Berlin Wall has come down. The unimaginable has become commonplace. Movements that also call themselves revolutions—from the Soviet Union through what was once the socialist bloc of Eastern Europe—have defeated Communism in one country after another. In our own hemisphere Nicaragua's Sandinista revolution was voted out of office and a brief period of Haitian democracy was squelched by a military coup. Corruption and rigidity have surfaced. Old assumptions have cracked. But none of the governments replacing socialist or people's systems have been able to make life better for their populations. And in some of these countries—Poland, Hungary, Lithuania, Ukraine, and Slovakia among others—communist or socialist forces have made partial comebacks.

Still, the change hit hard. Suddenly everything is different. What we once called communist or socialist often wasn't either.

What the free market politicians call democracy is anything but. We may have polluted and politicked ourselves beyond retrieval. Today's wars shame the human condition.

I return to Havana deeply afraid. How much longer can Cuba's heroic experiment continue to resist: against blockade and isolation, the loss of international markets, and a succession of U.S. administrations waging fanatical opposition to Cuba's right to exist?

What follows are vignettes of Cuban life, glimpsed through the early-to mid-1990s. This is not a comprehensive view—a piece about what Cuba is. It assumes some knowledge of the revolution and does not offer up-to-the-minute statistics or in-depth political analysis. Rather, these are reflections of a process of change. I want to record what feels different, what the same. Given the situation of ravaging hostility and ongoing isolation the Cuban people have faced for 35 years, this is a piece about resistance.

My returns have been on two separate occasions[1] with groups of North American women, a broad spectrum of professionals and women in the trades, many of us political and community activists, some of us artists and writers. We represent a diversity of racial, class, sexual, and cultural identities. These have been feminist trips. We have been most interested in connecting with Cuban women and learning of their current situation, how they see themselves in society, the ways in which they feel their revolution has moved them forward or held them back.

What follows, as I say, are vignettes. They are not impartial. They are what I saw, heard, felt—tempered by my intimate knowledge of the Cuban experience, my children's memories and my own, and a critical eye developed through more than a quarter-century of involvement: joy, rage, pain, and an ever-deepening perspective on human struggle.

We meet with interesting people, often in settings too formal for our taste: the proverbial conference table rimmed with straight-backed chairs is a common denominator on these trips. This afternoon the people—women—are wonderful and so is the setting. The community, in Havana's greenbelt, is called La Guinera. For years it was home to impoverished working people living in crowded shacks.

The revolution has succeeded in giving all its citizens education, work, health care, culture, and recreation. When times are rough the necessities spread thin; when production goes up it divides fairly equally. Still, housing has long been one of the toughest problems to solve. People whose ration books give them access to a standard diet, women for whom the threat of cervical cancer has all but disappeared because they are given the same yearly pap smear as their more fortunate sisters, often inhabit painfully inadequate living quarters.

For the past thirteen years the women of La Guinera have been doing something about this. The *women* have been doing something about it, specifically the women. They were the ones who believed they could build these high-rises and ended up changing the face and character of their community. Fifí is an Afro-Cuban woman in her fifties. She greets us expansively and invites us into a common room: the workers' dining facility. An enormous photograph of Fidel stares back at us from the wall opposite the entrance. Immediately beneath this portrait is a table for eight set with white linen, expensive china, wine glasses, and a full compliment of forks, knives, and spoons. Later we learn that this is where the women have taught themselves to "eat correctly." "It came in handy in North Korea when I found myself at the table with Kim Il Sung," says Fifí, her face aglow with memories of the high spot on that trip.

On the wall to our left is a primitive mural: mountains, palm trees, a beach. To the right: smaller tables where the construction workers take their meals. Scattered around them or standing here and there are the women Fifí was able to round up for our visit, "so that you can see this project isn't only about me," she laughs. As we talk, in the circle of chairs that have been arranged in the only unfurnished area, she pulls one or another of them to her side, from where they contribute with their own stories of transformation. The local Party official and the People's Power delegate—both men—are mostly silent onlookers.

"There are thirty-three construction workers in each of our brigades," says Fifí, beginning with the work. "Nineteen build the apartments and the other fourteen work on social service structures: the schools, laundries, and so forth. A good sixty percent of us—and *all* the bosses—are women. We've finished nine of the twenty-two buildings we've projected. And we have an elementary school, a junior high, three special needs schools, a health clinic, a laundry…" she looks to the other women to make sure she hasn't forgotten anything. "There's the market," one of them adds.

At first statistics dominate the exposition. But gradually we get the women to speak about their lives. Initial problems with husbands who weren't prepared to take over at home while their wives went into construction. The pride this work has given them. The positive changes in the community itself. We are most interested in attitudes, the *process* of change these women have experienced, *as women.* Fifí responds to one request for an example of political work by exclaiming: "Why child, everything we do is political! Including meeting with you here today…"

Walking through the neighborhood and into the building sites is exciting. The women glow as they show us nearly-finished apartments. They are eager to explain innovations their crews have contributed. Both buildings we visit will be turned over to their new occupants within the following week, "as a salute to the first of May." Women stop shoveling cement or plastering or digging line trenches to chat with us as we come through. None of us wants to leave.

We are gathered in a large circle in the central patio of what the Santa Clarans proudly call their House of the City. Half museum, half meeting place, it is a lovely colonial structure being renovated for community use. The limitations imposed by the special period have clearly slowed down this renovation, making it more difficult. Still, those charged with the project don't lose hope. The crystal prisms on one of the great chandeliers have been replaced with graceful tubes of modern glass. On closer inspection we see they are the instruments used in cattle insemination! "This was an innovation," the historian showing us around tells us proudly. "We don't have enough electricity these days to do it the old-fashioned way. But these long glass syringes do give a similar effect."

Everywhere we have seen evidence of this new ingenuity, made necessary by the demands of the special period: Fidel Castro's designation for the still open-ended time, begun more than three years ago now, when Cuba's population was asked to intensify its already considerable level of sacrifice—their only possible recipe for "survival with dignity." In Santa Clara we take our seats in a large circle of old carved wooden chairs and the newer folding variety. Above us, across a square of evening sky, brilliant stars dot deep blue. It seems the city's entire political representation has come to greet us; we had expected to be meeting with local FMC grass-roots leadership and foresee a much too formal exchange.

Introductions begin. We note that a number of the women hold important positions in science, medicine, education, and the law. One heads the provincial psychiatric hospital, another is the president of the polytechnic university. One is a doctor, spoken of reverently by the others for her work for children with leukemia. There are several national politicians: a representative to the National Assembly (Cuba's legislative body) and a number of provincial Party people. Slowly it dawns on several of us: these women are overwhelmingly over fifty and the majority of those in high positions are also very black—a departure from what we've seen in Havana. Despite impressive progress, colorism as well as racism continue to be problems here.

Still, there are too many of us in the room: perhaps sixty or seventy. How will we get past the generalized questions, a few statistics, their pleas for and our commitment to working to lift the blockade?

Then it happens. One of our group, as she asks what effects they think prioritizing tourism is having on women's lives, produces a post card and hands it across the circle to the Cuban woman closest to her. The card features a very large foreground-image of a Mulatto woman's buttocks, perfunctorily covered by the splash of a brightly-colored bikini. The woman is standing in such a way that this part of her anatomy is thrust towards the viewer, almost entirely filling the picture plane; in the residual corners are bits of beach, surf, a couple of palms.

A Cuban woman takes the card, looks at the image, and seems confused. "Well," she says finally, "I don't see anything wrong with this." Instinctively she knows that we do. "Our women are like this, beautiful and sexy...this isn't something that started with the revolution." She passes it to the woman next to her, who in turn offers it to another. Everyone is eager to see this picture which so obviously troubles their North American guests. One after another, their comments attempt to laugh away our concern. A marked edge of defensiveness begins to grip the assembly.

After a number of women have had their say the provincial FMC's Secretary General takes the card in her hands. There is a brief silence. Then, without the slightest tone of patronage, with not a tinge of accusation, she says: "This is absolutely denigrating. Disgusting." Her discourse is deeply political. Rather than take an antagonistic stand, she builds upon words and phrases uttered belligerently by one or another of the women who commented before her. She will not personalize or shame. Yet her analysis of the offending image is thorough, implacable. And she reminds her sisters:

"We talked about these sexist images of women at our last municipal assembly. Remember? We spent more time on this subject than on any other. You were there [to one of the women] and you, and you. It's easy to get defensive, when these things are brought to our attention, especially by foreigners. But we must look at them honestly and find ways to deal with such affronts to our dignity."

In the meeting's feeling as well as in its format something important has shifted. A couple of the Cuban women who had previously defended the postal image now enter into heated discussion with their more conscious sister. We realize we are being permitted to witness the kind of ideological struggle that goes on everywhere feminism thrives. It is a privilege. A couple of hours later, when we've finished cool fruit drinks and received long-stemmed white lilies from our hosts—each of them offering a lily to each of us—we want to keep on talking. And we do, standing in smaller groups around the lovely old mansion.

By my second visit, some of the women writers and artists have agreed to meet with members of our group. The UNEAC, or Cuban Union of Writers and Artists, brings people together in a number of separate unions; there are writers, painters and sculptors, photographers, and those working in several other media. The unions function in the provinces as well but many of the better-known artists are still in Havana. Younger artists and writers belong to something called the Sáenz Brothers Brigade, named—as so many entities in Cuba are—after two young writers martyred in the revolutionary war. Even after 35 years women are still vastly outnumbered—at least on the influential union directorates and even among the membership.

This inequality has begun to change. A recent UNEAC Congress thought the issue worth addressing and when its sessions had concluded, a number of top positions were held by women. But a glance at just about any issue of either of the institution's important journals still shows mostly male work. It's a long hard struggle.

As we head for the beautiful old mansion in the Vedado section of Havana I have high hopes for this meeting. The women have told us they've notified absolutely every woman member. And Abel Prieto, the UNEAC's new president, is known as a man "of the new generation," himself a poet, someone of proven attention to difference, to making changes, to righting classic wrongs. Prieto is also a member of the Cuban Communist Party's politburo, the highest ideological body in the country. Naming him president of the UNEAC is a clear indication of the importance the revolution places on culture.

My old friend Mirta meets us at the mansion's gates. As our group straggles across the lawn to a large meeting room added onto the old house, I ask if any of the other Cuban women have arrived. "Yes," she says, "though not as many as I'd hoped for. Communication breaks down so frequently here. I personally sent telegrams to everyone, but…"

"Look," I tell her, "we'll have a worthwhile discussion with whoever there is."

None of us could have predicted how this meeting would unfold. Waiting for us in the spacious room are eight, maybe ten women—from several art forms. To our surprise there are also several men. We didn't ask for a women-only meeting but somehow imagined that's what we'd get. As it turns out, an expectation far too influenced by our own process and culture.

Abel Prieto himself greets us. He's been out of the country, has just this afternoon flown into town, and—"because of the importance of this meeting," he says—wants to be a part of it. What he and many of the other Cubans see as courtesy and respect quickly become the element that throws everything off balance.

Of course introductions take a while. They always do with groups this large. By the time we've gone around the circle we North American women are chafing to get down to ideas, feelings, experience. I believe our Cuban sisters are too. But Prieto decides that as president of the institution he needs to welcome us. His remarks are cordial—and succeed in distancing us farther from the ways women share. Translating, I find myself having to resist frequent temptations to soften a comment or make another less culturally inappropriate.

The other men get into it too. When one of our women challenges something Prieto has said, or challenges his habit of instantly responding to a question posed to one of the Cuban women, he or they tend to make matters worse. Explanation follows explanation, justification stumbles after justification. Some of the Cuban women simply fold. Others tell us we "don't understand, things are getting much better here. After our last Congress we…"

Finally one of our women stands. A no-nonsense African-American writer and anthropologist with long experience in this sort of exchange, she faces Prieto and speaks: "We are very happy to be here," she begins. "We deeply appreciate your hospitality. But we have come to speak with our Cuban sisters. It's taken a long time but in our country we've come to a place where when a woman asks a question of another woman the other woman responds. I'm going to have to leave this gathering because I have a prior engagement. But I want you to know that many of us consider it rude for this type of constant interruption to go unchallenged."

The men in the room are still unable to listen. To truly hear. Further explanation comes across like static: too many defensive jokes, too many knowing looks, too much evasion. Even the women are unable to deal with what has transpired. There is anger. There is embarrassment. But there isn't much communication. At least not then and there.

Much later we hear that the Cuban women discussed what happened among themselves. And with the men. "It's pushed us to address these issues, to engage in a whole new level of struggle," one of them writes.

It's hot, almost steamy, in the streets of this fast-changing neighborhood on the outskirts of Santa Clara. This, like La Guinera in Havana and similar projects in every Cuban city, is a multidisciplinary effort to radically alter people's lives. Here people lived in makeshift shacks. Drugs and idleness were beginning to take hold. Too many teenage girls were having babies. The revolution was not doing what it was meant to do.

Through a variety of processes, neighbors themselves become architects and designers, construction crews, social workers, and the liaison between their community and the professionals in a variety of necessary skills. We have already visited La Guinera in Havana so we're familiar with the several formulae by which the Cuban state provides the building materials and the people concerned the provide labor power.

Here, however, we have come primarily to visit a neighborhood clinic and to speak with a family practice doctor. Cuba's free and comprehensive public health system is among the best in the world, in many areas rivaling those developed countries that successfully care for their people's bodies and minds: Sweden, France, Canada.

By the time I had moved to Cuba, when its revolution was ten years old, medical, dental, and psychological attention had already attained an amazing level of efficiency. Major pre-revolutionary diseases had been eradicated. The country's infant mortality rate and life expectancy were similar to those in the industrially advanced nations. It was about the time I left the island that the Cubans began experimenting with the idea of health professionals who would live in the community itself, get to know its members, caring for them in wellness as well as when they became ill. I had heard this was working and was eager to see how it is organized. I also want to know how the special period is affecting people's health.

A doctor friend in Havana had told me: "We've been able to maintain people's caloric intake to date, pretty much at an acceptable level. What pushes them over the edge is the extra energy expended on pumping those bikes—Chinese models weighing 50, 60 pounds…" I tried to imagine what it would be like, during the frequent and prolonged electrical blackouts, to haul one of those unwieldy frames up four or five flights of stairs. We'd also been told about optic neuritis, a condition that has appeared in all fourteen provinces and seems linked to a vitamin deficiency. When I visited my old neighborhood in the capital, I'd seen the local family practice doctor making her rounds, distributing multivitamins to every man, woman, and child.[2]

Now, in this scrubbed community on the outskirts of Santa Clara, we are being greeted by a doctor who clearly adores his practice. He welcomes us into his tiny clinic, proudly showing us sparse examples of basic equipment as well as many makeshift items harnessed into service by need and creativity. Old-fashioned hypodermic needles, fresh from the sterilizer, lay in neat rows upon a towel. A rudimentary examining table stands behind a modest curtain. On a table in a corner, a small board catches the attention of several in our group. From it protrudes the model of a small tan breast, brown nipple erect and broken lines carefully dividing the sphere into quarters.

"I made that myself," the young doctor says, with a mixture of pride and chagrin. "It's not as soft as it should be...it was a piggy-bank before it was a breast! But it works well enough for showing the women how to do their self-examinations." We ask and are told that breast cancer is the second cause of death among Cuban women. "What's the first?" "Hardening of the arteries," the doctor says.

The grandmothers, many of them standing around or talking to us individually, tend a fertile garden out in back. That's where their wisdom and the culture's long-ignored traditional roots and herbs are being cultivated against the special period's privations. Now a group of new mothers have gathered with their infants on the clinic's little porch. They seem willing to cede their doctor to us a while longer.

Walking through this neighborhood's streets, which are lined with small two- and three-family dwellings rather than the larger buildings we've seen in other places, it is obvious how much a part of the community this doctor is. And not just the doctor, but the local police officer. The teachers. The social workers. They all live in the neighborhood, come to know its people and their problems. Participants in a program as humane as it is effective.

From the family practice clinic it's on to a day care center—the Che Guevara—in another part of the city. Here in Santa Clara, many community resources are named for the legendary Argentinean who gave his life to the Cuban cause and then to a dream of continental freedom. For it was here in this central province that Che's column outwitted the dictatorship's army at the very end of the 1956-59 war. The night before, our group had visited the city's Che Guevara Museum, an impressive structure on which thousands of men, women, and young people labored voluntarily. A couple of us had found ourselves fighting back tears in that museum; the words and images touched raw nerves of memory, placing us face to face with our own histories of struggle. Che was much more than a t-shirt in our lives.

We return to our microbus for the ride from clinic to day care center, still deeply moved by the doctor with whom we've spent the early morning hours. We are impressed with the love and ingenuity with which people struggling together are able to face enormous problems. The Che Guevara Day Care Center is an imposing edifice, housing several hundred children from one to five years of age. A small group of them greet us at the door in a formal rendition of Martí's famous poem about being "a simple person, from a land of sun and sand..." Beyond them, in the airy downstairs areas and classrooms, little ones are engaged in all sorts of activities—from word games to group song to directed or independent play.

We follow the director, assistant director, on-site doctor, and several teachers—all of them women—from room to room. And outside into ample backyard play areas. The children are uniformly well-dressed, clean, involved. As in such a conglomeration anywhere, most seem exuberantly happy; a few are unhappy or simply loners. All seem respected. Some play doctor or house, or listen to stories. I stray from the group, wanting to spend a bit more time closer to the various centers of activity. I cannot help but think of my own children—whose early years were spent in New York City, Mexico, and—in the case of my youngest—Cuba. And I think of their children, my grandchildren, now growing up in France and Mexico City.

These Cuban children are enjoying life. And they are enjoyed by the adults in whose care they spend their days. All of the day care workers are female, although we are told that the schools where they study have recently begun accepting men. "Not many enroll, though," the assistant director admits. "No," I say, "I imagine not." The explicitly separate gender roles so evident in Cuban society as a whole will need to be addressed at a deeper level for that to happen. At the Che Guevara it is clear that these roles are very much in place. Little girls are playing with dolls. Little boys are mostly playing the rougher games.

We are told there is an effort to make changes in this respect: "We encourage our little boys to hold the dolls," one of the teachers explains, "because they will need to know how to help care for their own children when they grow up." The emphasis is still very much on helping. No one speaks about small children needing male role models among their caretakers, or men having qualities to give to the care of small children.

Still, the State's concern for its youngest population is moving and impressive—especially in light of current limitations. Back at the family practice clinic we had seen a makeshift day care program in effect; a single specialist guiding local mothers in the care and education of children who, because their mothers don't work, do not have access to the more professional model.

"We have noticed a great difference in the readiness, creativity, and ability to learn among those children who attend day care and those who don't. The latter enter elementary school at a marked disadvantage. So we knew we had to do something to try to even things out, to give those kids whose mothers stay at home a better shot at doing well in school." This is the comment of a mother, beaming at her own and other children as our group watches this less professional attempt to get every Cuban child off to the start she or he deserves.

We have gone back to the Federation of Cuban Women's national office, that elegant old house in the Vedado section of

Havana. This time, though, we are not sitting around a polished conference table, North American women on one side, our Cuban hosts on the other. This time we are not trying to make the most of a formal meeting in a room where preserved crystal embraces larger-than-life-sized photos of Che and Fidel. This is a more intimate exchange. Three Cuban women have expressed a willingness to talk about "anything you wish." One is an old friend. We North Americans are four.

The conversation moves easily from one topic to another. Building upon women's feelings of identification, we linger longer on the questions that have no answers, the projects that didn't turn out as anticipated, the unmet expectations. Suddenly weariness invades one of the Cuban women's eyes. She speaks with a particular urgency. "I want to tell you a story," she says.

"This happened in one of the provinces. I work with the regional leadership and I was on one of my frequent trips to visit cadre in the countryside. After a long day's work I saw my provincial counterpart take a carefully-wrapped package from her purse. It was a sanitary napkin and she was about to wash it and boil it on the stove so she could use it again the following day.

"Our sisters don't go through this ritual only for themselves," the speaker continued. "When her period ends, she passes the precious napkin on to a friend whose period is just beginning. Women in the countryside these days have to share their most intimate supplies. This is what the blockade, the economic crisis, our whole complex current situation can mean in a Cuban woman's life."

There's the late-night visit with Arturo and Omaida. He writes prize-winning short stories, earns his living working in the film industry. She is a musicologist. They and their two young children live with his mother in a wonderful old house on the eastern outskirts of the city. Cojímar, this area is called: semi-country, sea-washed, and very quiet at this hour.

My obligations with the group relegate personal visits like

this one to the hours when most people are in bed. These old friends have been waiting though, and even the kids are awake—intent on homework at a large dining room table. The old woman, who comes out to give me a hug, offers the customary cup of strong sweet coffee.

Arturo and I talk about poetry. Years ago we belonged to the same lovingly-remembered workshop that met Saturday mornings under the old trees of the university campus. Now a story of his has just won a prestigious international prize offered by the Mexican government. Intellectuals like Arturo and Omaida might well live in Mexico now; a number of their contemporaries have taken that route, setting up temporary or permanent residence in places where life is a whole lot easier.

"Have you thought about it?" I ask.

"Of course we have. But no, we're not going anywhere. Cuba is our home," they both agree.

These old friends tell me how they bike into the city each morning, she riding on his handlebars. They are thinner than I remember them, by a great deal. The gasoline crunch is a heavy part of the crisis. "It's good exercise," Arturo laughs. Omaida says it was much worse a few months back. "Then we didn't even have fuel for cooking," she explains. "The kids would come home in the afternoon, change out of their school clothes, and go out looking for driftwood. We had to keep a big fire going in the patio out back. That's where we cooked."

Still, this family believes things will get better. "We made a lot of mistakes," Arturo says, "but things have opened up here. There's been a lot of discussion, a lot of reevaluation. The fall of the socialist bloc is the best thing that could have happened to us. It saved our revolution. Now we're thinking for ourselves. We're becoming more independent, more able to solve our own problems. I think the worst of the crisis is past."

Omaida and Arturo tell me they've never been happier or felt more creative in their work.

For at least a number of our group, feminists and lesbian feminists from the United States, it is extremely important that we meet with Cuban lesbians. On the formal schedule there is an item: "Thursday morning, 9 a.m. Visit to the National Center for Sexual Education." And following it, in parentheses: "includes meeting with lesbians."

This is a disappointment. We had not intended a formal interview, but rather a more casual encounter with women like ourselves. It isn't their sexuality we are interested in exploring, after all, but how they live, how they feel, what degree of official or unofficial prejudice they must confront. We needn't have worried. The lesbians do not show up at the National Center for Sexual Education, and the fascinating women who receive us are visibly surprised that such a promise had been listed on our agenda. Not to their knowledge.

Our meeting at the Center is excellent. We find out about the many and integrated programs Cubans are developing to imbue their entire population with a healthy and responsible attitude about sexuality. Including homosexuality. They begin in their day care facilities. Certainly a giant leap forward from the years I lived in Havana.

But we still want to speak with Cuban lesbians. In conversations with lesbians in Nicaragua, I remember the sister who studied at the Cuban Film School telling me about gay life on the island. "I *really* came out there," she'd said, "there was so much support. A whole parallel world!" On the other hand, homophobia and heterosexism within the Cuban revolutionary process is well-documented. There is a history. We need to know what life for homosexuals is like in Cuba today.

Mirta agrees to meet us at the FMC guest house where we're staying. She is a writer—of short stories, poetry, children's books—and professor of literature at the University of Havana. Currently she works as a special consultant to the president of Cuba's Union of Writers and Artists. And she's an old friend. After one of those initial encounters—in which women speak to one another in telegraphic bursts of shorthand, cultures colliding and merging in experiences shared—we agree we must get together again.

Our last afternoon we take Mirta with us to beautiful Santa
María Beach. The temperature is mild, a light wind keeping the
air from blistering our unaccustomed skins. The beach is filled
with Cubans and foreigners, many of the former hauling their
bicycles seaside and hoisting them on their shoulders once more
after spending some time in the blue-green water.

Some of our group heads straight for the ocean. Others,
more interested in conversing with Mirta, settle under a stand
of coconut palms. Two young men immediately try to pick us
all up. "Go on now," Mirta tells them, "we want to be alone, to
talk." It takes the guys a few minutes but they finally get the picture. And we continue our conversation of several days before.

"Life has gotten much better for us here, there's no question about that," Mirta insists. "But there's no real community.
No movement as you know it. That's not viable, especially not
now." Mirta agrees that homophobia and heterosexism in Cuba,
like everywhere else, is profoundly linked to the patriarchal
model, and to the failure to grapple with feminist issues generally. Ironically this means that being a lesbian is easier than
being a gay man—precisely because women are less visible, in
their difference as well as in their more accepted social roles.

Mirta tells us that being gay in contemporary Cuba does
not stand in the way of having a home or a job—even the sensitive job of teaching (previously declared off-limits to homosexuals at a national educational conference in 1971, later
repealed). She and her ex-lover bought an apartment together,
"back when buying an apartment was something people could
do." It doesn't stand in the way of health care, which is assured to
every Cuban. But when I ask her about the recent breakup of
their twelve-year relationship she tells a story that includes pres-
sures not unlike those we suffer in the United States.

"My partner worked in Ethiopia for two years...the strain
of separation plus the stress of this special period...well, you
know how it can be." We do. I think of lesbian friends back
home, denied health insurance and other joint benefits because

their partners are not men but other women. Had Mirta's been a heterosexual relationship, provisions would have been made for her to accompany her lover overseas. In spite of the progress—won by movement struggle in our country, by growing official awareness in hers—both systems have a long way to go in really dealing with this most basic of discriminations.

We are gathered with another Mirta—a journalist—in her apartment in the Vedado area of Havana. She has created a wonderful spread from almost nothing and invited some friends to spend the evening with us: all women in some area of the media. All consider themselves feminists. There is a filmmaker. A sociologist who researches the lives of farm women. A television producer. An editor. A publicist. And a couple of women who write for the fast-disappearing written press (an extreme paper shortage during the special period has severely limited the publication of newspapers and magazines).

We ask questions of each other, our Cuban sisters as eager to grill us as we are them. "What about Hillary?" is one of the first tossed in our direction, as it has been at other meetings. Attacked and harassed by a long succession of U.S. presidents, the Cubans are naturally curious—and perhaps overly optimistic—about Clinton and his activist wife. We North American women concur in our fear that U.S. policy towards Cuba is not likely to change much with Clinton, at least not anytime soon. Some of us point out that the man is a member of the Trilateral Commission. And that Hillary's brother is married to a Cuban exile—active in her opposition to the revolution. None of this is news to these women, who are after all in a sophisticated field. It's their situation that pushes them to seek out any possibility of relief.

"How is the special period affecting women's lives?" we ask. "Have some women been forced back into more traditional roles?" A heated discussion begins then among the Cuban women in our midst. One rages against the term *special period*. "This isn't a special period," she insists, "it's a crisis. *A crisis, dammit!* We're never going to be able to deal with it until we can call it by its name."

Two of the women say they believe this period, "whatever we want to call it," is actually empowering women. "It's further socializing our home life," one of them says. "If a man comes home from work and he knows the gas is about to go off, maybe there's only fifteen minutes of electrical current left, he's not going to sit down and wait for his wife to come and start dinner. He'll do what needs to be done."

Not all our Cuban hosts agree: "Come on. Women's lives are much harder now," one of them insists. "It's just harder all around, harder to put food on the table, harder to wash clothes with so little soap, harder to keep the family in bare necessities. And you've got to admit it's we women who shoulder the brunt of all that. The double shift is something that hasn't changed. It's gotten worse."

The sociologist agrees. "We need to pay attention to what happens after," she says. "It may be true that some men will come home and get right to work rather than wait for their wives to make things happen. But what will happen after the emergency, after the special period? I think of Vietnam, where such a relatively high level of equality was achieved. Then the war ended and look what happened." She doesn't elaborate further.

I think of my own encounters with Vietnamese women towards the end of 1974. That was the fall I traveled through the soon-to-be-liberated North listening to women's stories. Again I see women with only a grade-school education, who learned complicated mathematical formulae in order to operate anti-aircraft guns in the coastal villages we passed through. I remember an elderly Women's Union cadre telling me how she traveled the countryside, teaching women to defend themselves against the rude abuses of their men. And I think of Nguyen Thi Binh—the Madam Binh of history—now Vice President of her country. When will we have a woman vice president of the United States? When will we have a woman president?

The openness and willingness to disagree we encounter in our discussion with Cuban feminists—indeed in all but the most formal of our programmed discussions—is also evident on the streets. Among strangers and friends. Opinions offered freely and with conviction. I have just paid a visit to my old neighborhood. Florinda and her several generations of family still live in their overcrowded little house squeezed between the apartment buildings on either side. Her husband, a butcher at the local supermarket, still wears a bright red flower behind his right ear. Her twin granddaughters are about to be graduated from high school; I photographed them in their starched school uniforms when they were just beginning first grade—and want to do so again.

They are surprised but happy to see me. Hugs all around. Almost immediately Florinda shows me six cakes of blue laundry soap: "Fifty pesos each," she says, not needing to add that she bought them on an active black market. Her ready complaints still ring in my ears from years ago. Florinda's daughter Antoñita—mother of the twins—points to a large pile of dirty clothes. "After six months we can finally wash," she says.

"And these," Florinda isn't finished. She brings out a couple of sad looking dinner rolls. "These were two pesos a piece." "Terrible times," chimes in Lidia, another neighbor who has easily lost thirty or forty pounds since I've seen her last. But we talk and she tells me her weight loss is not from lack of food. "I eat," she says, "but I'm so nervous." Stress has taken its toll in the special period.

As we reminisce about old times there is activity out in front. The neighborhood family practice doctor has arrived and sets up her little table and chair just off the sidewalk. Soon a line of neighbors forms. The doctor is distributing multivitamins (produced in Cuba) to every man, woman, and child. This is a government precaution, starting today, against the rash of optic neuritis. Later it is precisely this distribution of free preventative medication that prompts a middle-aged woman to stop me on the street a few blocks away and, after asking me where I'm from, to offer the following:

"You know, I sometimes think our government is too paternalistic; it does too much for us. Some of us could easily pay for those vitamins you see being distributed all over the place. (Current statistics show people in Havana with an average six months' surplus salary; in some other provinces the figure is lower.) Why not sell them to those who can pay? People will tell you we are suffering here. And it's true. These are hard times, especially hard because of your country's economic blockade. But we have the system we want and we'll defend it. You'll see…" I contemplate this woman, in her fifties or sixties, well-dressed and with enormous dignity. She carries a string bag with a couple of empty bottles, her billfold, and the familiar ration book. On her way to the market, I know. Why, I wonder, has she stopped a foreigner on the street, to offer an unasked-for opinion? For the same reason a half-block later a young man does the same.

"How does Cuba look to you?" he asks, clearly wanting to know. When I tell him I lived here in the '70s, that this is my first trip back and that frankly I am surprised—given what we hear—at the spirit of resistance I've found, he smiles grimly and says: "Yes. We still have the spirit. But don't kid yourself. It's all over here. We gave what we didn't even have for ourselves to people all over the world (he is referring to Cuba's internationalist missions). We have already begun to die."

This Cuban generosity—of opinion, trust, even material aid and goods—is characteristic. (An old man on the street notices one of our group wiping sweat from her forehead and offers her a bite of his water ice, served on a square of brown paper; no cones today!) I have forgotten how opinionated, energetic, and outspoken Cubans are. Or why the stories of "a silenced people" always come through so flawed. Even with their faces they are amazingly easy and free; Cuba is one of the few countries I've been where strangers actually seem to appreciate it when you take their picture!

We are at the Health Ministry's Health Education Center. A young woman and man receive us around one of those familiar conference tables. Of all their multiple health education plans, they know we are most interested in what is going on with AIDS: outreach, advocacy, treatment, and particularly the government's policy of hospitalizing all those who are HIV-positive as well as persons with AIDS. The approach is one Cuba has consistently defended as a logical part of its overall health policy: providing free and appropriate attention as efficiently as possible to an entire population.

The sanitoria—one in every province—have been visited by experts from all over. There is no question but that they are lovely places, offering a standard of living far above that enjoyed by most Cubans. Emotional as well as physical needs are met. The most up-to-date treatment is available. All of this is free and patients continue to earn the salaries they drew on the outside. Many of them have been going home on weekends or working outside the facilities. Still, for many of us the human rights issue remains: how does one equate obligatory residential care with freedom?

The staff at the Health Education Center tells us that to date, slightly more than 900 cases of HIV have been detected in Cuba (the country's testing program is extraordinarily far-reaching). Although some cases appeared among internationalists returning from Africa, the first seems to be traceable to a Cuban who returned from a visit to the United States. There are still more heterosexuals than homosexuals with the virus although the number of gay male victims has risen. A few children of both sexes have tested positive. Deaths stand at just above one hundred.

We are told about Cuban sexuality and how difficult it has been to make people aware. The programs are diverse and broad-based; from work with doctors and other professionals to programs at women's centers, in the schools, and among young rockers at a jamming place known as *El patio de María*

(María's Courtyard). The soft-spoken man answers a question about the availability of condoms: "No, like everything else here we don't have enough. We are distributing all donations. If we could get them in flavors we'd really like that—it would help with our campaign to tap into Cuban creativity!"

And then, without our even asking, the young woman responds to our unmentioned concern. "By the way," she says, "as of this month (May, 1993) we are no longer requiring patients to live on site. We believe we have done a fairly good job of reeducating our communities. Persons with HIV will be able to live at home if they so desire, continuing of course to get any needed medication or treatment at the sanitoria."

I am stunned—both at the information and at the casualness with which it's offered. Our news sources are so eager to feed us negative or troubling items about Cuba; positive policy changes are much slower to come to our attention. "Does this mean that the living facilities at the sanitoria are being closed down?" I ask. "No," she smiles, "only about half of the patients have opted to go home."

Religion—or spirituality—seems to have resurfaced throughout Cuban society. In a crafts shop the salesperson indicates a display: "These items reflect our African and Catholic syncretism," he explains. In a day care center two teachers wear small gold crosses around their necks. And at the art gallery of the Villa Clara Polytechnic Institute we are surprised by the power of several series of paintings. One is by a faculty member, the other by a student; both display strong Christian symbolism.

I remember how pervasive the materialist education my own children received here in the '70s was; and how frightened was my daughter Ana when at the age of ten we moved to very Catholic Nicaragua. Liberation theology has had its impact on Cuban revolutionary thought, of course, and over the past decade Fidel has spoken of the need for spiritual expression in several important interviews. Church people of many denominations have held conferences on the island; a group of forty-six

Methodists arrived on the same plane we did. On one of my visits, weekday morning mass at Havana's beautiful old cathedral plays to a modest attendance (about a fifth of the church is filled).

At its Fourth Congress, the Cuban Communist Party's acceptance of believers was an important validation for religious revolutionaries who had long felt a conflict between allegiance to their faith and to the revolution. What I observe tells me unequivocally that this is one of the changes that has successfully filtered down.

Another mandate of that Congress—decentralization—has been less uniformly easy to bring about. In the provinces of Cienfuegos and Las Tunas, I am told, young party and government officials with new energy and creativity have initiated programs that have made the special period much more bearable. In Cienfuegos, where most of the country's sugar is produced, pure ingenuity provides more accessible restaurants without the usual long lines. Popular fruit-drink stands have sprung up and all manner of recreation dependant upon recycling and a successful offensive against waste. There, they say, the average worker retains only seventeen days' surplus salary, as opposed to six months' worth in the capital.

As is true everywhere, what and how things get done often depends as much on the creativity of the people involved as on the political system that dictates policy.

A week before my second visit, the Cuban Institute of Cinematographic Art and Industry (ICAIC) hosted its yearly festival, a Havana gala. Directors, producers, actors and actresses, critics and people who love film reveled once again in the feast of Latin American releases. The Cuban revolution has created a film school in both senses of the term: in three decades it has developed a language in film that has been an important influence throughout Latin America and gained recognition worldwide. Quite literally there is also a school, a center underwritten in part by the great Colombian Nobel prize winner Gabriel García Márquez, to which aspiring filmmakers come from many parts of the continent and beyond.

At this year's festival a new Cuban production took top honors; aside from best film, *"Fresa y chocolate"* ("Strawberry and Chocolate") walked off with best actor, best supporting actress, best editing, and a host of other awards. In the current materials crisis only two copies of the film exist in the country; both were being shown commercially when we arrive and we notice lines blocks long from morning to closing. We want to see this film and several in our group make brave attempts, standing in line for hours. With our schedule, they never make it to show time.

I finally decide this is a picture we simply need to see. We must explore the possibility of getting passes; after all, we will be in the country too short a time to make waiting in long lines a viable activity. We feel awkward about asking for privilege, but the alternative is missing out altogether.

"Fresa y chocolate" is a film about the '70s. It explores a particularly rigid and dogmatic period in Cuban revolutionary history. That was the era of correct-linism, a clamp-down on critical questioning, and discrimination against homosexuals in particular and anyone considered "deviant" in general. It was a very painful period, for those attacked and also for those others of us for whom the attacks were felt as if in our own bodies.

"Fresa y chocolate" is the story of a young gay man who loves art and cares about Cuban culture. He tries to help a friend arrange a show of the friend's cutting-edge (and socially unacceptable) art. In the process he loses his own job; and eventually is pushed to believing there is nothing left for him in Cuba. He makes plans to leave his country.

Before he does, though, he tries to pick up a young man at Havana's Copelia ice cream parlor, an outdoor extravaganza of no little fame. The coded greeting revolves around strawberry and chocolate. Our second protagonist is a university student. He is not gay but his interest in literature attracts him to this man who manages to entice him home. The film explores their developing friendship, almost impeded by attempts on the part of the student's superior in the Young Communist organization to get him to keep track of the gay man's comings and goings.

Our hero refuses to be a spy. And *"Fresa y chocolate"* isn't just about heterosexism and homophobia in the Cuba of the '70s. It deals with other social fears as well: sexism, religious persecution, xenophobia, fear of difference. The film is beautifully made. It speaks clearly to outsiders as well as painfully—and redeemingly—to those who lived through these sad scenarios.

In the large Yara Theater every seat is taken. My attention moves from the screen to the audience and back. I am intrigued by the feeling of collective attention in that darkened space. Moments that would have wrung embarrassed laughter or catcalls from supposedly more sophisticated audiences elsewhere, elicit an electric attention here. When near the end of the film the two friends finally embrace, a ripple of audible relief runs through two thousand lungs in perfect harmony.

I emerge into the harsh light of a Havana afternoon convinced that however far the Cubans have yet to go in confronting their own homophobia, they are doing it and there is no going back. A revolutionary project if it is authentic must eventually include all social groups.

Friends tell me that "*Fresa y chocolate*" is not alone among the growing evidence of a greater openness to sexual difference. They talk about a soap opera (imported from Brazil) which was immensely popular the length of its sixteen-week run. The protagonists were a lesbian couple: healthy productive happy young women. When one dies her partner is grief-stricken. Before the end of the series she—and a vast Cuban audience—delight in her alliance with another wonderful woman.

On this same visit we are invited to a transsexual birthday party at a club in one of Havana's working-class neighborhoods. Only an unexpected electrical blackout keeps the party from happening. And then there is *El Menjunje*. It deserves my setting a proper stage:

We are in the middle of the island, in the province of Villa Clara. At a routine meeting at one of the FMC's Women's

Houses we're embroiled in fascinating discussion with professionals from a number of different fields: psychologists, lawyers, educators, social workers—they all donate a few hours a week to attend to the variety of problems women, children, and teenagers present.

A frequent question from our side involves wanting to know how sexuality is dealt with in the schools. What kind of sex education? When does it start? What about homosexuality? We receive the same answers we've gotten elsewhere: sex education starts with day care, it's mainstreamed into all the disciplines, and yes of course homosexuality is treated as a viable option. But then one of the women intervenes:

"If you're interested in homosexuality," she says, "I think you should stop by *El Menjunje*. That's our gay club here in Santa Clara. It's a wonderful place, open every night but Monday…and as late as there are still people dancing."

We glance at one another. No one has had an inkling that gay clubs exist in Cuba, much less in one of the provincial cities. A few telephone calls are made. Immediately we have plans to visit the place that night.

El Menjunje—the name means mixture, which is perfect for what goes on there—is located in the ruin of an old house in downtown Santa Clara. No roof, but the walls are inviting—alive with paintings, phrases, welcoming mottos. Cuba's climate is an outdoor one and the lack of a roof doesn't seem to be a problem. "Inside" there are tables, a small stage, an exhibition of poetry books, people dancing.

Those dancing are men and men, women and women, and women and men. This is community in the fullest sense of the word. Our group enjoys a long evening: music, drinks, even some food. Dancing, talk, a moving monologue dedicated to a young friend of those present who has recently died of AIDS. The next day I hunt down Silverio, the middle-aged gay man who founded the club and has been running it for the past several years. He welcomes me to his home and spends the morning telling me when, how, why:

"We would like to see places like *El Menjunje* all over the country," he admits, "but it takes so much work. Everything is so hard here now, with all the shortages…" I ask and he tells me he grew up poor, in the brutal Cuban countryside. A boy in a farm family, sober, hard-working. But his life became his own. He loved theater and eventually went to work in one. And he knew from an early age that he was gay.

"But we don't think of *El Menjunje* as a gay club," he went on. "Not in the sense I think you do. Our goal is to make everyone feel at home there: gay men, lesbians, and anyone else who likes to dance, loves poetry, theater, the arts. Party cards are usually given out at work places or schools, but the other night we awarded one at the club; the man was someone who spends a lot of time there. He's not gay, but he's a regular. And we knew that giving him his card at *El Menjunje* would mean a lot to him."

We talked. A few friends came by. They too became part of the conversation. We spoke of the arts, of how difficult it is in an economic crisis anywhere in the world to make sure people's spiritual and creative needs are met. "What can we do to contribute?" I couldn't help but ask.

Silverio smiled. "You may think it odd, but what we really need are a dozen kerosene lanterns. Sometimes there's no electricity and we have to close our doors. Last August we went a whole month without electricity in the evenings. It was sad. We couldn't stay open, and people really need what we have to offer. We can get the kerosene all right. But we need the lamps."

Things are changing, no doubt about that.

Once again I remind myself that this is not a visit on which I will be able to look up old friends. The demands of leading a women's trip must come first. If I begin to call people, I reason, I will only feel worse. But all good intentions have their exceptions. I cannot leave Cuba without being in touch with Martín. One of my oldest and best friends, he and I have a very special history: one drenched in laughter.

Juan Luís Martín is a sociologist with an executive position

at Cuba's Academy of Sciences. He is married to another sociologist, María Isabel, and has a 22-year-old son by an earlier
marriage. In the thirteen years since I've lived in Cuba our communication has been sparse—as it tends to be between Cuba
and other countries. So it takes a few phone calls before I finally
locate Martín. When we hear one another's voices on a crack-
ling Havana line we both dissolve into that old familiar laughter: raucous and warm.

Martín and I manage to spend one long afternoon together, as well as minutes stolen from a final evening. Again, it is
telegraphic communication as I rush through an account of my
own changes during these years: the time in Nicaragua, my
return to the U.S. and subsequent immigration case, my coming out as a lesbian, what each of my children is doing today.
And of course the grandchildren. We are driving to his home on
the edge of the city. "Should we go straight out," he wants to
know, "or stop somewhere along the way to talk?" "We have to
stop," I insist, noting that we are quickly approaching his house,
"because I want to hear about you as well."

Martín tells me about a second stint in Angola some years
back. About his work at the Academy: productive and satisfying. About his marriage. And of course about the special period. When I ask about his son Daniel a silence settles briefly
between us. We are parked by a lovely garden, great Banyan
trees shading the adjacent quiet. "Daniel has decided to leave the
country," Martín tells me. Tears come to his eyes. "You know
his mother has lived in Miami for years now. She finally convinced him to go."

"When?" I can feel my friend's anguish. "Next Thursday,"
he replies.

Martín now faces the intimate breakup which has been
such a tragic experience for many Cuban families. For him it is
the loss of his only child, a son he loves deeply. I want to know if
he has managed to stick by Daniel in this decision, to continue to
show his love even through his feelings of devastation. He
assures me he has. We cry together.

This is one of the casualties of prolonged hard times, perhaps also of the revolution's demands; Martín speaks of how often he was away from Cuba during the years of Daniel's growing up. His imminent loss brings to my mind and heart similar losses back home. More than a few of my friends' children have succumbed to the social problems of life in the States: drugs, joblessness, homelessness, depression, or generational estrangement. The terrible difference is that the Cuban revolution was made and is being sustained essentially for its children. Such enormous sacrifice: for the children.

Martín pulls himself together and we continue the drive to his home. His parents, who live in an older house in front greet me like old times. Daniel and I exchange pleasantries. Nothing is said about the boy's decision to leave. Then Martín and I continue back to the newer house where he and María Isabel live. This is semi-country. There are banana trees and chickens, an atmosphere of light, and good energy.

María Isabel has begun to prepare a sumptuous feast. She sends Martín out to pick a head of lettuce from their garden. "The special period hasn't been too hard on us food-wise," she says. "We have a garden like almost everyone else." I have seen these gardens throughout the country: from planters on the balconies of apartment houses and good-sized plots next to single-family homes, to the large communal efforts rimming multi-family dwellings.

Martín tells me they have 52 different vegetables, fruits, and herbs, all of which are doing well. Except for the white rice everything in the meal we share comes from this garden: a delicious black bean soup, Spanish omelette with potatoes and herbs, lettuce salad, and a platter of tastefully arranged tomatoes, carrots, asparagus, and purple onions. We enjoy a banana wine that tastes like vermouth; Martín makes and bottles it himself. Dessert is fruit compote: yes, also from the trees out back.

But if food is no problem, transportation is a hideous one. Martín tells me his gasoline ration allows him to drive to work ten days a month. And it is likely to become more restrictive.

The rest of the time he must take a bus, which—from where he lives—means *four hours of travel each way*. We're not talking about sitting on a bus, maybe reading a book to kill the time. No. These eight hours a day are spent squeezed into standing-room-only, sometimes hanging on. With the changes in the Soviet Union an extreme reduction in Cuba's oil imports has created enormous problems of this kind.

Martín and María Isabel, like everyone else who is able, use their Chinese-made bikes for shorter distances. "You must be exhausted," I say, impressed by the bus schedule I've just heard. "Of course," Martín agrees. "On days I can't drive, I get up around three in the morning. I leave the house by 4:30 and don't get home until 10:30 or 11:00 at night."

So what is the bottom line? What kind of general statistics are we looking at? Martín tells me that in the thirty-six months the special period has been in effect, Cuba has gone from the third highest standard of living in Latin America to the twenty-fourth. I try to imagine what this means in people's lives. "So far we have managed to keep the essentials," he says: "our program of public health, our basic food distribution, education, some small amount of growth in terms of social services.

"Last year we bottomed out," he continues. "We could only spend what we actually produced here, what we get from the sale of our sugar and other products. That was a terrible year; from one day to the next we went from the fairly good level we had achieved through so much work, to almost nothing. This year we were beginning to show a small increase in gross national product: from tourism and from the sale of pharmaceuticals. And then the storm hit."

What we called the storm of the century here—the blizzard that hit our eastern seaboard with such force in March—was terrifying tropical devastation by the time it assaulted Cuba. Winds of up to 125 miles an hour and heavy rains caused an estimated one billion dollars worth of damage; leaving 150,000 people homeless, destroying crops, and doing great destruction to industry, service centers, deliveries, and the like.

So as she has had to do so many many times before, Cuba was forced to pick herself up, assess the tragedy, and move on. All in the midst of an economic crisis that allows little margin for maneuvering. What has brought the Cuban people this far is what, for lack of a more explicit term, I'll call revolutionary spirit. In spite of what is being said and written about the country these days, my experience says there's still a heroic store of such spirit here.

Cuba is an island some ninety miles off the coast of Florida. After winning its freedom from Spain in the last years of the 1800s, it suffered more than half a century of economic dependency upon the United States enforced by local strongarm governments. Since the 1959 victory of Fidel Castro's 26th of July Movement, a succession of U.S. administrations have not ceased to attempt to destroy the Cuban revolution—by any means possible: from outright invasion (Bay of Pigs, April, 1961) to ongoing economic blockade, sanctions against other countries trading with the island, attempts on Castro's life, introduction of crop and animal plagues, Radio and TV Martí, and the most recent Torricelli Bill (which prevents ships wishing to dock at U.S. ports from delivering cargo to Cuba).

I returned expecting to find a nation in economic chaos, with a high level of collective depression and great numbers of people anxious to leave. I found depression, of course, and many who do want to leave. But I found a vast majority determined to stay, who support their revolution and its leadership through whatever the solution may be. This does not mean there is no criticism. There is a great deal. And Cubans—to their credit and the revolution's health—are extremely vocal in articulating all complaints and disagreements.

A friend tells me: "If we can make it through the next couple of years, I think we'll be all right." Some version of this pronouncement, which is also a great hope, is heard often. Many tell me they believe the world is changing and that some form of negotiation will have to be undertaken. "But our freedom is

203

non-negotiable," they add.

Homeward bound, as we make our way through immigration once more, people are saying goodbye. Cubans who are leaving—for a visit, or forever—and those who are staying. Some farewell scenes are particularly wrenching. I see someone who resembles the woman sitting across the aisle from me on the plane coming down. Was she coming or going? It all begins to blur, this repetition of family separations, and I wonder: what can possibly justify our government's Cuba policy? With the demise of the Soviet Union, what kind of a threat—in anyone's view—can Cuba possibly be?

Ninety miles off our shores is an island nation of almost eleven million people. For thirty-four years they have said with their lives that they want socialism, a system that puts people first. For thirty-four years, against extraordinary adversity, they have built their schools and their health system, eradicated hunger and unemployment, lowered their infant mortality to that of the developed world, produced art and poetry, made mistakes and rectified errors.

After our haunting debacles in Guatemala, the Dominican Republic, Vietnam, Chile, Grenada, Panama, Iraq, Nicaragua, and so many other places, will we—the American people—be able to say no to U.S. government policy in Cuba? Will we ever be able to defeat the blockade?

—Summer, 1993–Winter, 1994

Notes

1. April-May and December, 1993. I have led women's trips of feminist inquiry, traveling with groups ranging from 14 to 24 women each. They were organized through Global Exchange of San Francisco, California and Cuba's Federation of Cuban Women.
2. After this writing, and through the program of making vitamins available to everyone in the country, the epidemic was eradicated.

Index

About the Author

Margaret Randall is the author of more than 60 books. She was born and raised in the U.S. and lived for twenty-three years in Mexico, Cuba, and Nicaragua. Having relinquished her citizenship when she married a Mexican, she was denied U.S. residency when she returned to the United States in 1984. After a five year fight, she regained her citizenship in 1989. She lives in New Mexico.